Praise for *Unu*

"King hits the nail on the head with the true
times no outlet for help, support or counse   ... ... tactics that we
BIPOC leaders can take with us into the workplace. Real life stories have great applicability. An easy read with great takeaways. A book I will share with my mentees as young emerging BIPOC leaders."

—Denzil Ross, CEO, Northwest Medical Center Houghton

"Many books today tell the reader about issues related to diversity, equity, and inclusion in the workplace. Others describe leadership and professional development techniques. *Unwritten Insights* does a masterful job of weaving these important, timely, and essential challenges together, using the rare and truly special experiences of the author as examples. This is an important contribution to the field and will enhance the careers of many and lead to organizations where all can thrive."

—Christy Harris Lemak, PhD, FACHE, Professor, Health Services Administration, University of Alabama at Birmingham

"WOW. This book is right on the mark! It is an honest assessment of the challenges that people of color often face in corporate America. While we would like to believe all people are treated the same, the truth is, people of color are often judged differently, and this can impact performance as well as promotions and other opportunities. *Unwritten Insights* will help you navigate those real life situations. It provides tangible solutions for surviving and thriving in corporate America."

—Debby Ballard, Retired Executive, Sprint

"*Unwritten Insights* is an impactful look at what it takes for BIPOC leaders to succeed in today's dynamic environment. Lenetra King brings into the open the unspoken challenges and unwritten strategies to successfully navigate them. This book should be an essential read for all BIPOC leaders and their allies as we work together to open leadership opportunities for all."

—Aaron Bujnowski, FACHE, Healthcare Strategy and Leadership Expert

"*Unwritten Insights* is a powerful book that outlines the rules of the game. Lenetra's vast experiences, coupled with executive interviews, give a much-needed resource and guide for those who want to advance in corporate America. As an ally, I learned tools to help me as I mentor and sponsor Black students and professionals, and I will be recommending it to my colleagues as well. If you are serious about seeing more Black leaders in the C-Suite and boardrooms, read this book!"

—John Crossman, CCIM, CRX, President, Crossmarc Services, LLC

"As we live forward, it is often through reflection and review that we gain key insights. Lenetra has distilled many years of reflection and experience into this literary work. Her story openly shares the untold, a stark reality, and gives hope. I believe you will find inspiration and guidance in this playbook. Expect to become more impactful!"

—Ron C. Hamilton, Senior Vice President, Global Head, Reinsurance Governance & Operations Services (reinsurance industry)

"The vulnerability and grit displayed within the first eighteen pages had me hooked. You knew the woman that went through this journey had some jewels to share with us. And share she did! This book will leave you 'excelling'. . . with real life, tangible practices that you can put in place right away to help advance not only in your career but in life overall. Thank you so much, Lenetra, for creating the playbook we didn't know we needed."

—LaTosha Miller, Executive Director (global financial services firm)

"*Unwritten Insights* unleashes the . . . codes that every aspiring leader needs to reach their true potential. King eloquently shares golden nuggets of wisdom around the importance of sponsorship and coverage that we all should have and, more importantly, give to others."

—Tequila Smith, EVP/Chief Sustainability Officer, Covanta

"*Unwritten Insights* is a playbook for corporate leaders of color, regardless of years in the industry, that's informative, well-crafted, and well-implemented—a blueprint for winning. Lenetra King did a spectacular job and was able to leverage her extensive industry experience, education, and passion in an effort to change the balance of power in the corporate space. I highly recommend this book as a must read."

—Freddie Raines, Veteran Corporate Business Banking Manager, Senior Market Sales Executive (banking industry)

"*Unwritten Insights* is the book we always needed but didn't have. From discussing how to navigate the corporate political landscape to taking a deep, proactive approach to personal development and ultimately building a brand that is sustainable and successful, Lenetra fills in the blanks. Taking cues from her masterful career and strong network, *Unwritten Insights* lays the fundamental building blocks of career progression that are applicable to everyone from entry level to the C-Suite."

—Brandon J. Handy, Vice President, Global Talent Management, BBB Industries

"*Unwritten Insights* is a great compendium of the business challenges faced in the BIPOC community. This book couples real world experiences with detailed analysis of what many BIPOC face in the competition for recognition and advancement in the corporate world. The exciting part is that *Unwritten Insights* takes that next step of providing action steps to address the obstacles! I highly recommend reading this engaging accumulation of insights that can grow any person interested in advancing past the identified barriers to career progression."

—Michael Luckett, Senior Director (specialty retail home goods industry)

UNWRITTEN INSIGHTS

UNWRITTEN

Insights

A CAREER PLAYBOOK *for* LEADERS *of* COLOR

LENETRA KING

VIVE
PRESS

FORT WORTH, TX

Watch Me EXCEL® Press
Copyright © 2022 by Lenetra King. All rights reserved.
Paperback ISBN: 979-8-9868730-0-8
eBook ISBN: 979-8-9868730-1-5

Library of Congress Control Number: 2022920767

Poem by Ross Cooper on page 196 reprinted with permission.

Book cover design by Erin Seaward-Hiatt
Interior design by Christina Thiele
Editorial production by kn literary

UnwrittenInsights.com

To professionals of color everywhere who desire to show up unapologetically and unequivocally as their most authentic selves: brave, brilliant, bold, and ready to change the world.

Yes, this book is dedicated to you!

CONTENTS

"LIFT EV'RY VOICE AND SING"

Lift ev'ry voice and sing,

Till earth and heaven ring.

Ring with the harmonies of Liberty;

Let our rejoicing rise,

High as the list'ning skies,

Let it resound loud as the rolling sea.

Sing a song full of the faith that the dark past has taught us,

Sing a song full of the hope that the present has brought us;

Facing the rising sun of our new day begun,

Let us march on till victory is won.

Stony the road we trod,

Bitter the chast'ning rod,

Felt in the days when hope unborn had died;

Yet with a steady beat,

Have not our weary feet,

Come to the place for which our fathers sighed?

We have come over a way that with tears has been watered,

We have come, treading our path through the blood of the
slaughtered,

Out from the gloomy past,

Till now we stand at last

Where the bright gleam of our bright star is cast.

God of our weary years,

God of our silent tears,

Thou who has brought us thus far on the way;

Thou who has by Thy might,

Led us into the light,

Keep us forever in the path, we pray.

Lest our feet stray from the places, our God, where we met Thee,

Lest our hearts, drunk with the wine of the world, we forget Thee,

Shadowed beneath thy hand,

May we forever stand,

True to our God,

True to our native land.

—James Weldon Johnson

"Bringing the **gifts that my ancestors gave, I am the dream and the hope of the slave**. I rise. I rise. I rise."

—Maya Angelou, poet and civil-rights activist

INTRODUCTION

*O*ne thing is certain: for leaders of color[1] to excel at what they do, hard work and talent are great—but they are never enough to garner the highest pinnacles of success.

Have you ever felt stressed about your job? Do you feel like you're not progressing? Maybe you feel like you're doing everything you can or should, but you're not seeing the benefits of your actions. *Unwritten Insights* lays out a playbook for winning in the corporate environment game; it provides insights that took me years, along with a few missteps, to figure out on my own.

BIPOC leaders have a special relationship with our careers and our place at the leadership table. Some of us have come into our roles by sheer virtue of getting the education, doing the work, and receiving recognition for our efforts. Others, no matter how much education we have or how many all-nighters we have put in, seem to be unable to advance demonstrably in our careers. We face a host of obvious and not-so-obvious challenges when it comes to rising to the top of our game and receiving the support and external validation that truly mirror our excellence back to us.

This book explores some of the "unwritten" rules in the proverbial playbook for succeeding as a leader of color. I've distilled these tips primarily from the vantage point of corporate America, but they will be just as pertinent to leaders in other sectors, from

---

1 Throughout this book, I will use the term *leaders of color* interchangeably with *BIPOC (Black, Indigenous, and people of color) leaders*. (Although the abbreviation BIPOC is primarily a noun, I have also chosen to use it as an adjective.) However, the majority of my examples come from firsthand research on the experiences of Black leaders. The interviews I conducted for this book were also with Black leaders (although I include the insights of a few White allies). While my hope is that all leaders of color will gain valuable tools from this book, I chose to focus on Black experiences, given both the body of research illustrating the disparity between opportunities for Black versus White leaders, as well as the severe underrepresentation of Black leaders across a wide selection of industries. Because the Black experience has spearheaded awareness of racial inequities in North America, my hope is that all people of color will resonate with and find inspiration in the examples I provide throughout this book.

nonprofit to government, and even to leaders who are bootstrapping entrepreneurial start-ups.

There are a number of reasons I wish to pay it forward to current BIPOC leaders as well as future generations. My impetus for writing this book is to offer guidance to other leaders of color as well as to those allies who stand up and support us. I wish I had known some of these nuggets of wisdom that could have prepared me for everything I had to face during my corporate career as a Black woman, who more than once was the only Black woman executive at the table.

I am very familiar with the struggles many leaders of color face, especially early in their careers. I felt this acutely, despite the fact that I had a comparatively auspicious and promising start. I attended Florida A&M University in Tallahassee, Florida and am forever grateful for the foundation that this historically Black college/university (HBCU) gave me for entering the workforce and adulthood. However, at many stages throughout my career, I often felt I lacked the vital skills to help me play the chess game, make savvy moves, and maintain a sense of integrity and purpose in a competitive corporate environment where BIPOC in executive leadership roles weren't exactly commonplace. I wondered if other aspiring leaders had somehow received a manual that helped them intricately move the pieces on the workplace game board, and I simply hadn't been privy to it!

At some point, I realized there was no playbook for BIPOC leaders—which may be the reason so few professionals of color hold critical executive leadership roles at major companies. Although most of us are aware of the need for diversity and equal opportunities, data reveal that the number of BIPOC leaders, especially Black ones, is still depressingly low when it comes to sitting on boards and in C-suite roles. CNN notes that in 2018 "Black professionals . . . held just 3.3 percent of all executive or senior leadership roles . . . according to the US Equal Employment Opportunity Commission." Further, "among Fortune 500 companies, less than 1 percent of CEOs are Black . . . and over the past two decades, there have only been 17 Black CEOs in total."[1] As I write this in 2022, only two Fortune 500 companies are led by Black women![2]

Unwritten Insights is for all BIPOC leaders, especially those who keep raising their hand to advance but have been overlooked, for those who haven't had access to mid- to senior-level roles they are clearly well qualified for, and for those who are still trying to find their way in a space where there is no one who looks like them, especially at the top of the organization. If you can relate, please know that you're not alone. Many leaders of color, including those whose experiences are shared throughout this book, live by the adage that "we must work twice as hard for half the recognition," and almost always for much less pay.

I know so many talented BIPOC leaders who are dealing with and have been carrying the weight of generational traumas: healthcare inequities and lack of access to primary and specialty care; communities in the urban core and rural areas that have food deserts, poor educational systems, and high crime; a lack of infrastructure that supports upward economic mobility; and more. However, all of them still managed to overcome such inequities and build beautiful, purposeful lives. People of color have the skills and the resilience to accomplish remarkable things—we simply need the visibility and opportunities to show the world what we've got.

Having spent almost two decades in the hospital industry, and more than half of that time as a C-suite executive, I wrote this book for leaders of color around the world who are in search of guidance and practical tools for leadership and career success. My hope is that you will learn from the valuable lessons I, and other people I know, have culled over the years.

This book is intended for those who have felt stuck or have

struggled to figure out why they aren't progressing in their careers in a way that is proportional to the energy they've been expending. Because BIPOC leaders face unique challenges when it comes to navigating the workplace—especially with respect to the intersectionality of race and gender in predominantly white and male environments—this book is a much-needed guide that will help you to succeed and continue to grow in the workplace and beyond.

The book offers a blueprint to help you advocate for yourself—as well as learn how to help others advocate for you, even when you aren't in the room. Part one highlights the challenges leaders of color face, and part two provides the playbook. While the chapters in part two each focus on a specific rule, they also include two or more insights that shed light on how you can utilize the information I've offered to manage the nuances of leadership competencies and help you move your career forward. Topics include personal branding, bringing your authentic self to work, cultivating a strong executive presence, and creating a foundation for meaningful relationships that will support and uplift you throughout your career, including the ever-increasingly important roles of mentorship and sponsorship.

As you work through this book, you will come across real-life examples that you can apply to your own situation. Although this work is not exhaustive of the unwritten dynamics of a workplace, it is a stepping-stone meant to start turning the wheels of thought as well as spark dialogue between you and your village of supporters.

My Story

Let me tell you a little about my background so you'll know why I am so passionate about the topic at hand. I grew up in a small Alabama town where everyone knew everyone else. I was born to a teen mom and raised in the house with my grandmother who worked at the local hospital, about twenty minutes away. By the time my grandmother retired, she had worked for close to thirty years at a minimum-wage job as a tech in the operating room.

When I was growing up, life was challenging. I was at somewhat of a disadvantage in terms of life skills and exposure. However, what we lacked in exposure, my family more than compensated for in their love for each other and the value we placed on family. My grandmother was the matriarch; her drive, selfless sacrifice, rock-solid work ethic, and sheer determination to give me every opportunity under the sun to "make it" had an undeniable impact and influence that shaped who I am today. She is part of the reason I chose a career in health care.

As a first-generation college student, I attended Florida A&M University in Tallahassee, Florida, where I majored in health care management. After graduating from FAMU, I worked for a few years and then pursued graduate studies in health administration at the University of Alabama at Birmingham. As part of the degree requirements, I had to participate in an administrative residency under the preceptorship (a mentored experience) of a hospital CEO. After I finished my didactic studies, I moved to Kansas City, Missouri, to complete my residency at a large, urban core Level 1 trauma center (a comprehensive hospital that provides care for severely injured patients). Although I didn't fully appreciate the experience until years later, during this time, I reported to a Black hospital CEO—a true rarity in the early 2000s. It was from this CEO that I learned the importance of driving results, having strong business acumen, being politically savvy, and managing complex relationships with key internal and external stakeholders.

After completing my residency, I moved into entry-level management, and a year later, transitioned into an executive support role to work directly with the CEO I mentioned earlier. Over the next two years, I was given tremendous opportunities for learning and applying theoretical skills, as well as seeing firsthand healthcare inequities, as the system provided a significant amount of uncompensated care to residents in the Kansas City area. My time with this CEO shaped me indelibly and cemented in me a passion for advocating for the underserved.

I ultimately decided to move to a new organization to gain deeper operations experience —this time, on the for-profit side of health care. I applied for and was accepted to the highly selective chief operating officer development program (COODP) with a Fortune 500 hospital management company. To give you a sense of the selectiveness of the program, we were told that there were more than 800 applicants for only eleven slots for the cohort I was selected for! Within the healthcare industry, this particular company had a very strong reputation as being fiercely competitive in the markets where they had hospitals, so they were known as being an exceptional training ground to learn hospital operations.

Once accepted to the COODP, I moved to New Orleans to be the associate administrator at an academic medical center. You may recall Hurricane Katrina hit and devastated the area in 2005. The hospital where I went to work was the first such entity to reopen in Katrina's aftermath; thus, I had the opportunity to eat, live, and breathe in that city during a time of tremendous rebuilding. These years were some of the most memorable of my life. At this hospital—and under a CEO who gave me responsibility, autonomy, and opportunities to lead, contribute, *and* fail with his support—I learned many hard lessons. One of them was that, as a young African American healthcare executive, having "cover" from a more senior executive sponsor was necessary and critical for my career success and advancement. When I talk about *cover*, I am referring to the role my sponsor CEO played not only in accelerating my growth and development, but also in giving me the necessary bandwidth to make decisions, even bad ones, and supporting me when I failed. He "leaned in to" my development and supported me fully.

I ultimately took on executive-level oversight of the two campuses of this hospital system as vice president of operations.

Two years later, I was promoted to my first hospital chief operating officer role, once again in the Kansas City area—this time, for a boutique community hospital in the suburbs. This was my second stint in Kansas City, where years earlier, I had started my career at a safety-net trauma hospital that served the underserved in the city's urban core. This time in my career, I was at a hospital that served several of the wealthiest zip codes in an enclave across the Kansas state line. After close to five years in that role, I returned to the nonprofit side of healthcare, joining the flagship hospital of a large regional health system in North Texas as vice president and professional services officer. There, I continued to refine my operational and leadership skills, and I learned more critical life and leadership lessons. It was during this time that I was asked to join my first hospital community board of trustees, so not only was I in operations leadership, but I was also learning board governance in the hospital space, which was a very humbling moment for me career-wise.

I had been in the role and with the organization for approximately two years, when I was asked to meet with the system's chief operating officer. Before this, I had never met with this individual one-on-one and interacted with him only on a few occasions in group settings. So, of course, this summons was nerve-racking. I arrived at the office, wondering what I had said or done *this* time to get me a meeting in *this* office. After some small talk, though, the chief operating officer asked me to consider a role on his team: a newly created senior-level position in which I would be senior vice president and channel leader (think of channel as a division) and where I would have enterprise-level responsibility. He went on to say the position had already been posted, and if I was interested, I would need to review the posting and apply for it. However, I had the opportunity to go into the role on an interim basis. The reason I call this out, as we will talk about later in this book, is the value of driving results, managing my personal brand, as well as sponsorship were all at play here.

I grappled with the decision for a while, mostly due to my own self-doubt. How would the commute be, which, on a good day and in good traffic, was probably forty-five minutes? Would I join a team of other dynamic leaders? Would they like me? How would I measure up? Would I be working all night and all weekend to keep up? And on and on and on. Being a wife and mother of a young son, I was also thinking about the impact on my family dynamics and whether I could "manage." With some hesitation, I left everything that had been comfortable up to that point—hospital operations—and jumped into the unknown of a newly created senior leadership role in a corporate office.

I went into the role on an interim basis for approximately six months, then I put my hat in the ring by applying and going through the interview process for the permanent position. Two months after I was named the permanent leader, the person who had advocated for me to fill this role passed away—yes, two months into this brand-new role as the permanent leader. I felt as if my world had turned upside down because I lost a key advocate in this new role. I was transferred to a new leader and new team; then, the COVID-19 pandemic hit in March 2020, and life as many of us knew it changed dramatically. Working from home and not the corporate office became my reality.

Another world-shattering event occurred that spring with the murder of George Floyd. As a Black woman in senior leadership at the time, this atrocity hit me in ways I cannot adequately express. Suffice it to say, it was a challenging time personally and professionally, and I had to come to grips with where I was going to stand on this side of history. As with so many other leaders of color I knew personally, who were also dealing with their own feelings of how to manage the civil unrest and balance it with still showing up at work and performing through the comments and the questions, it became a time of deep introspection about my own life, career, and path forward.

During this time, I launched my company, Watch Me EXCEL®. It was a way to marry my passion for entrepreneurship, leadership equity, and uplifting high-achieving women and men of color in corporate spaces. I also wanted to partner with organizations who had committed dollars to advance their diversity, equity, and inclusion imperatives by developing and equipping their leaders with tools to enhance their own capabilities and thrive in corporate environments.

After an organizational realignment occurred, I transitioned out of the corporate world and into my business on a full-time basis. And today, as I write this, I am dedicating my passion to creating transformational leaders who are supported in showing up as their best selves. I feel grateful that in this work I get to advocate for equity in a more meaningful way that I wasn't able to do in previous incarnations of my career—mostly because it was challenging to pursue this while working for other corporations, and I often felt the weight of the "golden handcuffs." Additionally, my work as an entrepreneur gives me the flexibility to be there for my family in a very different way: I can control more of my schedule and destiny while enjoying the time with my son during his formative lower school years.

It's important for me to push equity in spaces where people of color work—both on the front lines as well as in leadership roles. I want to be instrumental in helping create environments and institutions where all of us can feel psychologically safe—and where we know, without a doubt, we belong and have our seat at the table.

You Have What It Takes—You're Not Alone

Although I've shared a bit of my story with you, I haven't gone into the many peaks and valleys I navigated over the years—from discovering my own strengths as a leader and developing strategies to support hundreds of other team members to missing critical cues relative to managing complex relationships. Nor have I scratched the surface when it comes to the ways that race and gender have intersected to define my journey through the corporate world. Over the years, I've befriended strong allies who helped me define my goals, maintain my integrity, and display excellence and resilience even in moments of adversity.

Now, I want to be that kind of ally for you. If you've ever felt stagnant, confused, or blocked on your trajectory as a leader, it is absolutely possible for you to move forward with greater clarity and confidence in your abilities. Our society still has a long way to go to create equitable systems that offer more and better opportunities to people of color. But as we continue to make individual strides in our careers, we can pay it forward and use our own experiences to raise up other leaders of color and help them step into their excellence.

No matter what you've been through—both the triumphs and challenges—know that you have everything within you to succeed. My hope is that the rules in this playbook will help you remember just how awesome and capable you are. You've got this!

Unwritten Insights is my way of paying it forward and offering guidance and encouragement as you expand your ideas of what's possible. I want to help you understand what it takes to navigate exceptionally in spaces that have been historically white. As you read this book, please imagine me right beside you, cheering you on and championing your strength and special gifts. The world needs your unique voice and leadership. I've got your back, and I know that supporting BIPOC leaders can be a catalyst for the kind of change we need to see in our world.

Are you ready to be the change you wish to see? If so, keep reading!

PART 1

THE ENVIRONMENT LEADERS OF COLOR FACE

The **way to right wrongs** is to **turn the light of truth** upon them.

—Ida B. Wells-Barnett, journalist, educator, and civil-rights activist

CHAPTER 1

Why Cultural Competence Matters in Today's Corporate Environment

*W*hat is cultural competence? Why is it important? And what are the characteristics of a leader who displays it?

The answers to these questions have expanded and evolved across most industries over the past few decades. The following description of *cultural competence* summarizes the practice well. It is a continuous and lifelong journey to increase people's skills in being proficient in intercultural and intracultural knowledge, which can improve the ability to work with people [of a] different culture.[1]

In other words, cultural competence entails the ability to understand and interact with people from a variety of backgrounds and cultures. It requires having a general understanding of your own culture and how it has shaped you (rather than assuming that your culture is the default, shared by everyone), as well as the willingness to accept and normalize cultural practices, behaviors, and worldviews that might be very different from your own. Cultural competence is about moving beyond "tolerance" and into genuine respect and acceptance.

For leaders and organizations to remain relevant, especially during this time of turmoil, constant change, and expanding globalization, cultural competence is not an option. It must be a work style that is leveraged among all leaders and ingrained into the core of every mission, vision, policy, process, and decision.

Georgetown University suggests "five essential elements contribute to a system's, institution's, or agency's ability to become more culturally competent."[2] These include:

1. Valuing diversity
2. Having the capacity for cultural self-assessment
3. Being conscious of the dynamics inherent when [different] cultures interact
4. Having institutionalized culture knowledge [the set of shared assumptions, values, and beliefs that preside over how people behave in organizations]
5. Having developed adaptations to service delivery reflecting an understanding of cultural diversity[3]

Many leaders of color have been directly impacted by a lack of cultural competence in the environments in which they've nurtured their careers. It can be painful to enter a room where your identity and culture are minimized and where you are expected to conform to the default leadership or executive norm—which in many cases is overwhelmingly white and male. This standard is often placed on us unconsciously, which is why it is so important for all leaders to recognize how they can set a positive example—by acquiring the skills, knowledge, and attitude to ensure more welcoming environments for people from different cultures.

Many industries have been slow to recognize why cultural competence is so important, and they tend to perpetuate a "business as usual" mentality that requires many of us (especially BIPOC) to leave certain parts of our identities at the door, or, with the hopes of being accepted, de-ethnicize our identities to fit in. However, cultural competence is a powerful quality in today's workforce; a lack of it negates opportunities to build relationships.

Since it is a leader's responsibility to set the tone around inclusion, how can we continue to reinforce cultural sensitivity and awareness throughout our lives and careers? We can start by being honest about the aspects of another culture that are unfamiliar to us. Regardless of whether we are familiar with the culture or not, we can practice respect at all times and avoid assuming that everyone else must fit into the box of our preconceived notions. We also have to be receptive to the possibility that understanding a culture may not happen immediately; however, respect is a key first step to opening more transparent communication, as well as sincere and well-intentioned curiosity to learn something we might not already know.

As a leader, if you listen closely to your team, you can start becoming aware of its different cultures and paradigms. If you are a leader who has chosen to sponsor another professional (which we will discuss in greater depth later in this book), you can represent them much more effectively when you have become competent and attuned to the cultural norms in which the professional operates.

This book focuses on equipping you with skills and insights that will serve you throughout your career, and cultural competence is at the top of the list. I also am sensitive to the allies and other professionals who are not leaders of color, and I want to ensure we are all working from the same understanding about cultural competence. Being a leader of color doesn't automatically mean you are better equipped than white leaders to practice cultural competence (although, in many cases, this might be true). So, I want to explain some of the terms we'll be using throughout this book to drive home the importance of creating and being part of an inclusive work environment—especially if you have run into experiences in your career that have been the opposite.

- *Diversity* includes all the ways in which people differ, encompassing the characteristics that make one individual or group different from another. It includes not only race and ethnicity, but also gender, age, national origin, religion, disability, sexual orientation, socioeconomic status, education, marital status, language, and physical appearance.
- *Equity* is fair treatment, access, opportunity, and advancement for all people. When equity is in place, we also strive to identify and eliminate barriers that have prevented the full participation of some groups. In the workplace, we can respond to certain questions that enable greater equity for everyone, especially the most marginalized among us:
  1. How do you improve equity in the workplace for leaders of color?
  2. How do you create equitable access to leadership positions for everyone?
  3. What are the systemic barriers that prevent leaders of color from equitable access to mentorship, sponsorship, and visibility opportunities?
  4. How do more leaders of color get recruited, interviewed, selected, and hired?
  5. How do you break down the root causes of lack of access to leadership roles?
- *Inclusion* is the intention of creating environments in which any individual or group can be and feel welcomed, respected, supported, and valued in order to participate fully. To be inclusive means displaying and having a genuine curiosity about people. An inclusive leader understands that biases remove an individual's distinctiveness. For example, if you hold underlying discrimination against a person who lives in a particular geographic loca-

tion or associates with a specific political party, your preconceived notions erase their potential and the qualities
that make them shine.

- *Parity* is the state or condition of being equal, especially
  when it comes to status and pay.
- *Belonging* is the often unspoken aspect of cultural competence. In many organizations with DEI (diversity, equity,
  and inclusion) initiatives, there isn't necessarily a concerted
  effort to help people of color feel that they truly deserve
  a seat at the table. For example, although I held many
  high-ranking positions within the organizations where I
  worked, I didn't always feel that I "belonged." In speaking
  with other colleagues, especially those I interviewed for
  this book, I found I am not isolated in those feelings of
  lack of belonging. It isn't enough to fill quotas and do
  more outreach in underserved communities. It isn't even
  enough to promote a culture that is actively anti-racist
  and that works to address biases. We need more organizations that are willing to do the work to ensure that all
  people feel *psychologically safe* and invited to be their
  whole selves while at work. When organizations have this
  as a mission, then leaders of color can truly operate from a
  place of authenticity and realness through a cultural lens.
  And, as many of my colleagues agree, when we are able to
  do this *authentically*, we can be more effective in our roles
  leading others.

When we learn to practice the various components of cultural competence, we truly create a greater sense of team cohesion
and genuine inclusivity in the workplace. Historically, so many
workplaces and industries have failed people of color by creating
exclusive hierarchies that were never intended to include them.

Cultural competence is a powerful corrective because it defines the principles and beliefs we have about cultural differences and experiences, and it turns these beliefs into tangible policy. It allows us to walk our talk, so to speak.

When we practice diversity, equity, and inclusion, we start to build work cultures where everyone can thrive. In order to do this, we have to acknowledge our blind spots as well as the overall social inequities that still impact marginalized people, especially talented BIPOC who clearly display leadership abilities but have not been afforded the same opportunities to excel. While this is usually unintentional, many organizations have not created level playing fields for everyone.

Most of us have direct experience with the ways unfair advantages and opportunities have given some people privilege and power over others. Although we may not have the same social advantages as other groups, simply acknowledging the importance of cultural competence can help us set goals toward greater equity.

In today's world, we are beginning to recognize the importance of amplifying the voices of BIPOC, especially with changing demographics and the imperative to serve more diverse communities. After all, a lack of cultural competence can make us lose out on the rich resources and experiences that come from diverse backgrounds. It can also harm both individuals and populations who are underrepresented or not represented at all in boardrooms across the nation where key decisions are being made.

Overall, cultural competence gives us the ability to envision new possibilities and new ways of leading that boost appreciation of both our similarities and our differences. Moreover, it provides the kind of stable foundation that will allow leaders of color to flourish, whatever environment they find themselves in.

The **most powerful ancestral or generational curse** we face is our **unhealed trauma**.

—Abiola Abrams, writer

CHAPTER 2

Implicit Bias, Microaggressions, Racial Trauma, and Their Impact on Leaders of Color

*Y*ou might be wondering: If awareness of cultural competence's importance is growing in corporate environments, why do we still see leaders of color struggle? Why do BIPOC leaders still need to work twice as hard, sometimes reaping only half the rewards, compared to our white counterparts?

Of course, many of us know that overt systemic racism and discrimination continue to be an issue, but in many corporate environments that purport to be more inclusive, leaders of color face an unspoken epidemic of implicit bias and microaggressions that can stand in the way of getting to where they want to go. Let's look at each of these in turn.

Implicit Bias

Implicit (also known as *unconscious*) *bias* can be defined as "bias that results from the tendency to process information based on unconscious associations and feelings, even when these are contrary to one's conscious or declared beliefs."[1]

Thoughts and feelings can be considered implicit when we are simply ignorant that they exist in the background, or we're mistaken about where they come from. A bias results when, instead of being neutral, we display a preference for (or aversion to) a specific person or group of people. Thus, implicit bias describes the attitudes we have toward people or stereotypes we associate with them (Asian people are good at math; Hispanic people can't speak English; Black people are lazy), without even being consciously aware of this.[2] Implicit bias also extends to the unconscious ideas we internalize from language; for example, whiteness tends to be associated with qualities like goodness and purity, whereas blackness gets tied to dirtiness and evil (think about terms like blackmail, blackballing, blacklisting, and the phrase "the pot calling the kettle black"). All of us use these words and terms without even realizing what they imply, or how those subliminal beliefs are affecting us currently and have been affecting many of us for generations.

Leaders need to be aware of implicit biases because it can be more challenging to uncover them than overt racism and obviously negative stereotypes. Implicit biases are the undercurrent of thinking patterns and processes that must be undone. They affect decisions unconsciously, which is why they are so pervasive. Additionally, people tend to hold on to their biases because, due to mental laziness, it is easier to go to battle for an untruth than to address one's own missteps. Although many more people are doing work to uncover their implicit biases,[3] for some the mere topic can bring up a great deal of defensiveness and a litany of reasons to justify their behavior instead of owning up to something that could be corrected with deeper reflection and a sincere desire to do better.

What are some of the pervasive implicit biases that exist in the workplace? According to an April 2021 report from the US Bureau of Labor Statistics, 57.4 percent of women participated in the labor force in 2019.[4] While the past year has seen an increase in the number of female CEOs at Fortune 500 companies, there were only forty-one female CEOs accounting for 8 percent in the nation's highest-grossing companies.[5]

Why the discrepancy? Many reports have suggested that

implicit and explicit bias could be behind it. Some chilling statistics suggest that people believe men make better political leaders and business executives than women.[6] Another study found that, in the United States, 57 percent of respondents held a gender-biased belief, and more than 30 percent had more than one gender-biased belief.[7] While it may not be necessary to obsess over these statistics daily, it is essential for leaders to take action and do their part to unhook from gender biases. As a palpable example of how to do so, following are some responses you can integrate into the workplace to support gender equity.[8]

- **Challenge the stereotype.** As a leader, have you found yourself questioning the advancement of a woman on your team because she has two children at home? Have you made the assumption or decision that a promotion will be too much for her to handle along with her home responsibilities? If so, take action to actively challenge these stereotypes and replace them with more positive and uplifting expectations and mental pictures. If you notice pejorative attitudes toward women—especially BIPOC women, who face both racism and sexism—from other leaders, address them directly. Sometimes, a simple "What do you mean by that?" can work wonders.
- **Examine hiring and compensation practices.** During hiring, if a woman interviews for a position typically held by men, imagine how a woman leader would positively impact the department and the company. Share your perspective with other influential people within the organization. Additionally, evaluate the compensation structure at your organization to ensure that women are paid equally and commensurately with males in the same roles and with similar years of experience.

- **Individualize.** Gather specific information about an individual woman rather than making generalizations based on her gender. For example, perhaps you know of a working mother in your department who resigned because she wanted to place all her attention on raising her child. As a leader, you must understand that her reasons for leaving were specific to her and do not apply to other working women in the department or on your team.
- **Create increased opportunities to network with women to discuss their ideas and visions.** This action ties back to the importance of individualizing people and their decisions. Allowing a platform for women to discuss their ideas and concepts openly reveals uniqueness.

For BIPOC leaders, implicit bias carries even more adverse consequences because it is tied to the harmful effects of systemic racism. Systemic racism, "(also known as structural racism or institutional racism) refers to systems and policies that harm the health and livelihood of BIPOC."[9] The systemic nature of racism makes it easy for implicit biases to continue. A 2020 report revealed that "nearly one in three Black employees (32 percent), one in four Asian employees (23 percent), and one in seven Latinx employees (15 percent) say they feel out of place at work because of their ethnicity."[10]

BIPOC leaders endure stress because they are often viewed as exceptions to the stereotypes placed on them. An article by Enumale Agada beautifully illustrates what the author refers to as the myth of black exceptionalism:

> It's the notion that black people who are educated, smart, articulate, poised, and basically every other positive adjective you can think of are atypical or rarities among the general black population. So what's wrong with this

notion? Well to begin, educated, smart, articulate, poised, etc. black people are not rarities or exceptions. They may seem to be exceptions based on the biased and unflattering depictions of black people that run rampant in the mainstream media (it seems that we've been upgraded from maids and butlers to angry black women and thugs), but they are not. This notion of black exceptionalism also bears the underlying assumption that there exists a single and one-dimensional manifestation of blackness. A black person that does not conform to this imposed, sole image of blackness is somehow an exception to the rule. In creating this false dichotomy, the myth of black exceptionalism denies us the individuality and the full spectrum of humanity that is so readily offered to the white population in this country.[11]

BIPOC leaders work under the unforgiving pressure to avoid failure at all costs because they are the "chosen ones who got through to sit at the table," and some feel they have to represent their entire race. This leads to exhaustion, perfectionism, burnout, and isolation—as well as the feeling that there is little support or empathy for what they are facing. The constant pressure to prove oneself can take a toll, and this undue stress—an invisible burden that may not be recognized by an employer—can lead to adverse results. On top of all this, the intersection between race and gender can create an additional double whammy for BIPOC women, who may face biases that white women, white men, and men of color do not.

So, if companies want to retain high performers and not risk losing them to competitors who are serious about creating opportunities for BIPOC professionals, advocating for and implementing practices that create racial equality must be a central theme. Whether it's to generate tangible outcomes that work to significantly increase promotions granted to BIPOC leaders, or increase the participation and involvement of allies who want to advocate on behalf of BIPOC, policies must pave a path forward to more culturally competent and equitable workplaces.

Also, as BIPOC leaders, if we genuinely want to be positive change agents who are seeding transformation through our own actions and behaviors, we must be willing to uncover our own unconscious biases. Admitting we have them can be troublesome, especially if we've been on the receiving end of racial prejudice. But choosing to ignore our findings can have a domino effect on our relationships. When we ignore or deny our own biases, it affects how we view our teams and how we evaluate others. Instead of evaluating someone based on facts, we provide feedback based on our own hidden biases that we haven't chosen to face. These unaddressed prejudices and stereotypes gravely hinder inclusivity.

How do you know if you have hidden biases? First, you have to be willing to get uncomfortable. The following questions present a guideline for identifying the red flags that highlight the biases and stereotypes within your personal paradigm. [12]

- Do I think "all," "every," or "they" about a specific group?
- Would I say the same about another group?
- Do I rationalize, thinking a certain person is an exception?
- Do I base my evaluations on someone's actual behavior, or am I evaluating only on the basis of my opinions, judgments, and assumptions?
- Where and how did I learn my assumptions, biases, and stereotypes (from friends, family, media, personal experience)?
- Suppose I had a past personal experience that was negative with a member of a particular group. Do I expect or believe that all future experiences with this group will be negative?
- Do I have internalized racism or sexism shaped by larger cultural attitudes? That is, as a BIPOC, do I engage in discriminatory thoughts or behavior against other BIPOC?

Or as a woman, have I been indoctrinated to think of or behave poorly toward other women?

Asking ourselves these questions is not a one-time event. It takes constant truthfulness, and we cannot allow our assessments to be riddled by guilt and self-judgment, or by the idea that we can't be biased if we ourselves are people of color, as this will further hinder progress.

Microaggression

People of color are often faced with microaggression, "an action or statement that may seem innocuous but is considered by a person or people belonging to an oppressed group to be harmful because it displays racist, sexist, or otherwise bigoted attitudes and assumptions."[13]

One of my interviewees for this book, a Black senior vice president, noted that prior to the COVID-19 pandemic, he frequently traveled internationally for business. During one such trip while he was seated in first class, "I had the airport attendants say to me, 'You know this is first class.' My first response was, 'Yes, I'm aware.' So, why is there this assumption that I can't fly first class?" His experience is a glaring example of a microaggression, which can come off as harmless at first glance but points to deeper biases on closer examination.

Microaggressions extend not just to race and culture, but also to age, sex, and disability. However, for the purpose of this section, we're focusing on the many examples of racial microaggressions that BIPOC leaders face in corporate life. Unfortunately, microaggressions have become a part of everyday conversations and behavior, which is why so many BIPOC leaders can share specific examples, regardless of their position within an organization.

Microaggressions have largely been ignored and dismissed as

a minor flub or violation with no intent to harm. For decades, we didn't even have a name for this particular form of violence. The act is often reduced to something someone should "just get over and deal with" on his or her own because, after all, the comment "was just a joke" or "no big deal—you're blowing it out of proportion."

How *micro* is a microaggression? Let's look at some examples that play out in corporate America with respect to culture and race.

- "Where are you from? I mean, where are you *really* from?" This question is often asked of people with darker skin tones, who may be perceived as foreign.[14]
- "You are so articulate," or "You speak really good English." BIPOC leaders and professionals have reported receiving this "compliment" from colleagues who appear to be surprised by their exceptional communication skills.
- I have personally encountered individuals who, when speaking to someone of a different race, adopt an unusual accent or use a colloquialism they wouldn't typically use.
- Several Black women I know (and many others I have read about or am aware of through my colleagues) have experienced the violating incident of having their hair touched, or received disparaging or intrusive comments about their hairstyles, including that their hairstyle is "unprofessional." I vividly remember a conversation with an individual who reached out to me on behalf of her Black colleague who wore braids. This person was upset that her colleague had been asked how often she washed her hair. The person who'd asked her the question worked in human resources—talk about a lack of serious professionalism and tact from someone who should have known better!

These four examples of microaggressions do not begin to scratch the surface of those that persist in the workplace. Whether you have been on the receiving end or have found yourself committing the "micro" flub, let's look at what we can do to avoid making a microaggression.

We must all understand that recognizing a person's culture and race is to identify a part of what makes them unique. I have heard people tout the phrase "I don't see color." That may or may not be true, but it does not speak to your awareness of your own biases that lead to committing a microaggression. Moreover, the declaration of color blindness can be extremely dismissive of the very real, racially based differences in experience that people of color encounter on a daily basis. It can be a way of "invisibilizing" the very factors that have formed their sense of self in the world.

Leaders must also understand that proximity to another person of color does not mean that a person is privy to or understands their racial experience.[15] As I've mentioned, leaders must be dedicated to listening to people's stories in order to learn, even if understanding the experience does not present itself immediately. Also, before asking a person a question, or making a comment or comparison, take a moment to pause. This will allow you time to consider the potential impact of your words on the other person. After all, while a microaggression can seem "harmless," there is a growing body of research that suggests a lifetime of receiving microaggressions can negatively impact a person's mental health, leading to increased anxiety and symptoms of depression.[16]

Racial Trauma

The term *race-based traumatic stress* was first used by Robert T. Carter in his 2007 paper titled "Racism and Psychological and Emotional Injury: Recognizing and Assessing Race-Based Traumatic Stress," published by *The Counseling Psychologist*.[17] Carter's paper stipulated that when people of color encounter racism and discrimination, it has a strong negative emotional impact, and may be similar to post-traumatic stress disorder (PTSD).

As you might suspect, based on how seriously and intensely it can manifest, racial trauma's impacts are far-reaching. It leads to lower self-esteem and self-worth. As a glaring example, the trauma of witnessing repeated acts of police brutality leads people of color, particularly Black people, to fear police, which can in turn be dangerous if they find themselves in situations where they need to rely on police assistance. Racial trauma can cause severe emotional problems, such as dissociative symptoms. Overall, racial trauma can impact every facet of life, reducing significantly one's quality of living.[18]

The experience of Black people in the United States is one that is deeply affected by trauma. It has been found that traumatic historical events influence how cultural norms are passed down by older generations. Overall, findings suggest that it is extremely important to consider the effects of trauma on one's expression of emotion, and, for Black people in particular, exposure to trauma is an unavoidable aspect of our experience in society.

How does all this translate to the workplace? Unfortunately, if you are a person or leader of color, I would venture to say that at some point, you've had to cope with the impact of seeing or even personally experiencing continued injustices, all the while being expected to show up to your workplace with a smile, your true feelings safely tucked away. This kind of cognitive dissonance surely has lasting impacts.

This reminds me of a candid conversation I had with a CEO of a major company when giving him my feedback regarding my experiences of being a Black executive. I told him that I cannot hide my blackness when I show up to work, and that this was very different from his experience as a white man. He could leave the office, drive around the city, and even go to retail establishments without fear of being followed by security or of freezing when he saw a police car because he wondered what might happen if he got pulled over. He didn't face the constant dread of seeing news of violence committed against another Black woman, man, or child killed senselessly. I also shared that I could never escape being a Black woman and that, before anyone in the office saw me as an executive, they would always see a Black woman first. Additionally, as a Black mother, the fear and worry I carried about the world in which my son was being raised was more than enough to cause undue stress.

He met all of this with a long moment of silence—which I internalized as he was processing my words carefully, didn't understand them, or maybe didn't *want* to understand them. To this day, I am unsure which. At the time, I understood very clearly that the emotional labor I had put into having this very conversation would likely get me nowhere, but I felt deep in my core that I had to say what I'd said for my own peace of mind. I know racial trauma is real—and this is something that all leaders must be conscious of if they wish to understand clearly its catastrophic impacts on BIPOC leaders in the workplace.

How Racial Bias Holds Back Leaders of Color

From the examples just cited, it's not hard to determine the role that implicit bias and microaggressions play in the everyday lives of leaders of color. These biases can be the unacknowledged elephant in the room—and a severe impediment to our progress.

Systemic racism is all around us, and discrimination can happen in overt ways, but many of us are dealing with a more insidious form of racism when it comes to implicit bias and microaggressions. For many BIPOC leaders, it can be difficult to give voice to these experiences, especially in environments that say they value diversity, while their hiring, promotion, and compensation philosophies reflect a different practice altogether.

Although we may have come a long way, we have far to go. We are still living within systems created generations ago that were meant to minimize the advancement of BIPOC in every sector of life—from housing, education, and retail access, to availability of healthy foods, health care, and employment opportunities.

Many BIPOC start to experience these disparities at an early age, beginning with the treatment they receive at school. For example, Black students are punished more frequently and severely than their white peers, even though comparative levels and frequency of misbehavior are the same. While white students might be more frequently disciplined for "objective" misbehavior, such as vandalism, Black students are more likely to be punished for more "subjective" infractions, including loitering or acting disrespectfully.[19]

Harmful racial stereotypes can occur despite a marginalized person's efforts to make someone else (often, a person from the dominant culture) comfortable. Many times, BIPOC leaders, including the ones I interviewed for this book, have discovered that despite their best efforts to set other people, especially white people, at ease, their actions are routinely misperceived. A Black male healthcare executive I spoke with shared: "It's very easy for me to be stereotyped in the workplace. I am a tall Black man with a deep voice. I've heard multiple times that I'm intimidating just by nature of my physical attributes. I remember a time when I was doing some administrative rounds in the hospital. There were two doctors in the hallway who were conducting their clinical rounds on patients. Because of where they were standing, I slowed down and said, 'Excuse me.' That's all I said. 'Excuse me.' And a young lady who was in the hallway turned around, looked at me, and said, 'Oh, I'm sorry,' and stepped to the side. Several hours later, I got a call from HR. I was told that one of the doctors on the unit complained that I barked at her student. Now, I am not sure where that came from, but by me saying excuse me and walking through, they took it as me being aggressive." Although the executive shared that this incident didn't derail him at this one hospital, many other leaders of color have expressed the feeling of treading on eggshells because they don't know if, how, or when their differences might be construed as threatening—to the extent that they could harm their future career opportunities.

Although I have never personally been labeled as being aggressive, I have had similar experiences. Until fairly recently, I kept my employee badge in my car to ward off knee-jerk suspicions that have been leveled toward me as a Black woman. Several times, I've intentionally worn my employee badge inside retail establishments because I needed people to see that I was a senior-level executive who didn't need to be followed around the store by clerks or by security! Sometimes it worked, but sometimes it didn't matter. Security would follow me anyway, or I felt the suspecting stares from the retail workers. That was traumatic in and of itself. I was well aware of all the measures I needed to take simply to feel safe, accepted, and deserving of shopping in certain stores.

As mentioned in the previous section, racial microaggressions impact BIPOC negatively by compromising our mental health, creating physical ailments, decreasing productivity and the capacity to problem solve, and enabling hostile work climates. It's no surprise that BIPOC in the United States face glaring disparities, and these environmental factors carry over into the corporate environment—no matter how confident and resilient the leader of color or how "tolerant" and progressive the workplace.

In this way, communities of color deal with unique differentials "including economic disparities, institutional disadvantages, and experiences with racism/bigotry."[20] There is the burden of "racial battle fatigue" that can be described as "the extra mental and emotional burden" that negatively impacts a person of color "independent of their educational status, occupational role, or income."[21] The extra mental burden results from witnessing and being on the receiving end of the housing, politics, finance, labor, criminal justice, and education racial inequalities.

Unfortunately, the following statistics reveal that organizations still do not have an adequate understanding of how racial battle fatigue impacts people of color.

- Blacks reported a 60 percent higher rate of discrimination compared to whites.[22]
- Black employees begin their careers making less than their white colleagues, which leads to Black professionals receiving promotions less often. Biases also interfere with starting pay, future wages, and promotions.[23]
- As of October 2020, unemployment for Black Americans stood at nearly 11 percent, compared to 6 percent for whites.[24]
- Nearly two-thirds of Black people reported working for an organization where they believe racism plays a part. More than three in four US employees feel that racism is a problem.[25]
- When it comes to job seekers, 3 percent more white people with criminal records receive callbacks than do Black people without criminal records. The gap is even larger when it comes to Black applicants without criminal records compared to their white counterparts without criminal records (17 percent versus 34 percent, respectively).[26]
- In California, the CROWN (Create a Respectful and Open World for Natural Hair) Act was developed to

prevent companies from discriminating against Black employees, and by September 2020, three states outlawed discrimination against natural hairstyles. These bills are a positive beginning, but they don't do enough to sufficiently uproot the systems that perpetuate racist assumptions about Black people's appearances and that uphold racially based standards around what is considered "professional" in the workplace.[27]

Some companies have shown efforts to understand why BIPOC leaders' experiences are so starkly different from everyone else's. Since the heinous murder of George Floyd, which occurred in May 2020, companies have committed or dedicated 200 billion dollars to increase efforts toward racial justice. A large portion of these funds is meant to provide affordable housing, lend in low- and middle-income and minority communities, community development, and greater representation of BIPOC within the organizations themselves. Financial institutions were responsible for the majority of this commitment.[28]

Although it is unfortunate that the tragic extrajudicial murder of a Black man has been the catalyst to propel greater awareness of the burdens BIPOC disproportionately carry, I know that I and other leaders of color are hopeful it will open more transparent conversation and solutions to a problem that has plagued us for far too long.

Allyship and Accountability

It is easy for leaders to say they are committed to their teams' career advancement, but continuing to make the "business case for diversity and inclusion" solidifies the establishment of a welcoming environment.[29]

According to the 2017 US Census Bureau, the nation's population has and is continuing to become more diverse at rapid rates.[30] For businesses to continue to sustain themselves and remain relevant, their workforce has to match the diversity in the market. Particularly in leadership, when the work environment coincides with the demographics of the clients and customers it serves, more space must be made for creative solutions. Increased diversity, equity, inclusion, and belonging mean that there are individuals on the team and in leadership who can relate because of shared experiences that give them a greater understanding of the products and services that will add value.

Both white and BIPOC leaders must become aware of behaviors that have been deemed both acceptable and unacceptable in the workplace. Leaders must be open to the fact that diverse people do have diverse communication styles, and the methods by which people make decisions will differ based on their backgrounds. Leaders also need to acknowledge that diversity brings expertise in ways that look different from what has been deemed acceptable or "professional" and we should, therefore, remain adept at initiating team-member collaboration, encouraging everyone to be involved, engaged, and authentic.

Assessing our workplaces with the insights we'll be exploring throughout this book can also enable us to advocate for other people of color and to demand that organizations demonstrate their commitment to developing and advancing women and BIPOC leaders by developing a clear strategy to offer them better opportunities and retain them.

It is important to note that, while organizations can develop solutions, leaders need to remain consistent in their support during interactions with their teams, and be confident enough in addressing biases and microaggressions as they occur. It is only until this happens systematically that we will begin to address the culture challenges that exist for many BIPOC in corporate spaces.

The next section of this book is intended to redress these situations and give BIPOC leaders the tools they need to prevail, succeed, and change the game for all people of color, no matter their circumstances.

———

PART 2

The Playbook

X ⟶ O

**REACHING SUCCESS IN TODAY'S
CORPORATE ENVIRONMENT**

"I have learned that **success is to be measured** not so much by the position that one has reached in life as **by the obstacles which he has had to overcome while trying to succeed**.

—Booker T. Washington, educator, first president of the Tuskegee Normal and Industrial Institute (now Tuskegee University)

HOW THE PLAYBOOK WORKS

A book dedicated to leadership would not be complete without a list of insights or critical capabilities for successful leaders to thrive in the workplace. As we delve deeper into how we can continually advance in our leadership roles, it is paramount we examine the fundamental traits an influential leader must possess that are even more critical for leaders of color.

Whether you are a veteran in your leadership role, new to your assignment, or just starting your career with an eye on leadership in your future, this next part of the book highlights specific, vital competencies essential for growth and for advancing your career.

To present this section in an organized and easy-to-read manner, each chapter in the playbook revolves around a specific topic; at the end of every chapter, you'll find a series of insights that offer a specific subtopic with valuable information I and other leaders of color have picked up through our own corporate journeys. Throughout the book, you'll also find stories from BIPOC leaders who share their experiences, as well as lessons they've learned—both through their adversities and their triumphs.

Before we move on, I want to share insights of one of the leaders I spoke with regarding the power of presenting a book like this to other BIPOC leaders, because I think her wise words can benefit us all. "The career journey is truly a game, and the game is played by unwritten rules. The challenge is trying to discover those rules early enough to mitigate possible derailment. As an outsider, sometimes the system will not make sense. . . . You can learn the technical things, but it's the leadership competencies that will keep [leaders of color] from getting the plum assignments and the promotions.

It is very important to know what these unwritten rules are within the construct of a broader system that is not always designed to help us develop, advance, and be successful in leadership."

My hope is that the next several chapters will provide you with the support not only to navigate the system, but also to begin changing it for others.

———

"You have to **know what sparks the light in you** so that you, in your own way, can **illuminate the world**."

—Oprah Winfrey, producer, actress, and philanthropist

CHAPTER 3

Owning Your Personal and Professional Development

Our personal and professional development looks different for each of us because our life experiences and career desires vary. However, they are part of the same continuum. Your life is fully intertwined with your capacity to lead; the common thread is how you show up, because this impacts how people perceive you and your management style.

It is important to continue evolving and stepping into more of who we want to become. As high-performance leaders, we understand how critical it is to elevate our own growth in all aspects of our lives. We must understand that it requires patience and needs to be approached with consistency and dedication. If we're going to be seen as experts, we must intentionally and consistently engage in enhancing our skill sets to perform optimally, get noticed, and advance our careers.

Leadership involves a level of self-awareness that removes the need to compare yourself or your journey with anyone else's. However, it is easy to get caught in the comparison game.

Even though I've already noted how personal and professional development are two sides of the same coin, let's talk a bit more about personal development. It is not a destination, rather a constant exploratory process of honesty and self-awareness that contributes to our total well-being. Whether favorable or not, all the decisions we've made in our lives came from a certain level of personal evolution. As we grow, we can no longer make decisions from the viewpoint of an earlier level, which is why personal development is so important. When you can understand why you have engaged in certain behaviors, it is easier for you to relate to other people. Personal development extends your insight into other human behavior when you know your own.

The process helps us integrate the positive aspects of ourselves into all segments of our lives. Allow me to use even simpler terms: Personal development guides us to be excellent human beings and live meaningful lives. It involves making essential behavioral changes. It is about recognizing old habits and beliefs that have contributed to our behavior in any situation. Before changes in behavior can occur and before we can replace old patterns with new and helpful habits, we have to be honest about what is and isn't serving us. We have to be fully aware of our responses and how we make decisions.

Personal development does not involve self-judgment. It is about recognizing who we are, allowing ourselves to become more, and realizing growth is supposed to happen. Often, behavioral changes occur in spurts or incrementally, or only in certain areas of our lives. It is not a destination; we have to remember that it is not a process we have to rush through.

Personal development can also reveal whether you are trying to achieve a dream or a career that no longer suits you. As you move through this journey, you may find that you want to change course, enter another career field, change organizations, or start a new business. (I've been there myself!) You can view personal development as an unfolding into professional development and as the foundation of an exceptional career, however you define that.

This leads to our discussion of professional development,

which takes you beyond university degrees. While you were obtaining degrees, you sat in a classroom, and someone gave you a syllabus and told you what to study. Depending on the university you attended, you may have received instructions that allowed you to complete independent studies that correlated to the industry you wanted to work in. As you advanced in your degrees, you may have taken courses where you collected data to build a case study, created financial and marketing plans, or similar business applications. These steps added to your purview and provided a foundation and framework for you as you entered the workplace. Some of these courses helped you advance in your jobs when you entered school and obtained advanced degrees. Even with the pillars of education, you probably found you still had to build your career. The career did not just come to you.

Before you let ambition drive you to achieve additional degrees beyond the undergraduate level, you should develop a professional plan, and this is especially important for an early careerist. This can be as simple as writing out your ideal workday, and it will assist you in pursuing projects and activities that align with your plans. A written career plan is your blueprint and your guide. It will even propel your personal self-development and lead to more self-discovery. Your plan will reveal any additional skills you need and which mentors you need to seek. It will also keep you accountable, allowing you to revisit what you have written to see if anything needs to be adjusted or wiped out completely. The plan's purpose is not to limit you to one career path, but to help you stay focused so that you do not accept a job or assignment that isn't aligned with what you want. Having this plan will instill confidence in you to affirm how you want your career to look. You will be able to define what career success means for *you*.

Professional development also requires network building, which we'll explore in various parts of this book. When you have invested in your professional development, you will attract the mentors you need. People are more prone to assist you when your initiative to help yourself is apparent. Reach out to those who have grown to levels in their career that you aspire to attain. At each stage of your professional development, it will be helpful to interview those people with meaningful and thoughtful questions to find out how they got where they are.

I still think back to my first healthcare leadership job, when I reported to a Black hospital CEO who was sharp and dynamic, and had incredible business acumen and a knack for managing relationships. It was in that particular environment when I realized being successful required navigating the corporate world in a very sophisticated manner. However, I didn't fully understand or appreciate the extent to which I had to do this until I went to another organization and entered a highly competitive executive development and training program.

Both personal and professional development require consistency. You cannot be a bystander in your own life and career. Leaders cannot encourage or influence growth among their team members if they themselves do not evolve. This is why I emphasize the importance of owning our personal and professional development. Are we personally investing in ourselves? Are we having conversations with the people we need to be talking to in order to gain valuable feedback? Our active engagement is required here —it is definitely not about being passive or waiting for great opportunities and realizations to fall into our laps. We must take an intentional approach to being the best version of ourselves.

x— Insight 1 → o

Have a Healthy Mindset and a Positive Attitude

Having the right mindset as a dynamic and high-performing leader is crucial to leadership success. *Mindset* is defined as "a fixed attitude, intention, or inclination."[1] Although a *fixed attitude* can be seen as rigidity or stubbornness, there is certainly a positive side that demonstrates integrity and fidelity to one's goals. Having the right kind of mindset as a leader has a lot of dimensions, and key among them is a positive attitude.

It has been said that humans notice all things negative or anything that could go wrong because our brains are wired to shield us from danger and circumstances that do not render good feelings. While we all have this negativity bias, an effective leader desires to lead meaningfully and cultivate what is best not only within themselves but also within their team and enhance their experiences of daily activities;[2] that effectiveness can only happen through sustained positivity and optimism.

Let's review the benefits of positivity and optimism. Both qualities promote social and intrapersonal well-being. They influence a state of contentment and a desire in people to do good for themselves and others. They also lead to executing a plan while increasing one's ability to explore possibilities.

A leader cultivates positivity by focusing on what is working well and understands that being optimistic does not equate with denying challenges exist. While leaders maintain their outlook, they should be mindful that others have certain personality traits that can make them less prone to adopting a positive mindset. Others have learned behavior that makes them focus on everything that is *not* working. While leaders can't force someone to think a certain way, they can influence an individual to view a situation through a different, perhaps rosier, lens.

Are individuals born with a positive attitude, or are positivity and optimism learned? While some people naturally have these qualities, positivity and optimism can also be learned. As a leader, you can review the benefits of positivity with your team and empower them to choose how to approach any problem. Positivity is like a muscle; it must be exercised, or it will atrophy. When a challenge is foreseen, guide your team and employees through a simple activity, such as rewording a negatively written sentence into a positive statement.[3] This could look like changing "What is wrong with you and how can we fix it?" to "What is right with you and how can we promote it?" This simple activity can build up anyone's positivity muscle over time and optimize not just your performance, but also your capacity to stay open to solutions and possibilities.

x– Insight 2 → o

Take the Stage as a Confidently Charismatic Leader

An impactful leader emanates presence. According to social psychologist and bestselling author Amy Cuddy, "presence manifests its qualities as confidence, enthusiasm, comfort, being captivating."[4] So, what do you exude?

As executives, our presence—the way we dress, look, speak, and act—influences how others perceive us in the workplace. We must also be highly effective at asking the right questions and providing compelling input at the appropriate time. Confident leaders have exceptional relationships and social capital and are quick to manage their emotions. It is no secret that someone with confidence can inspire others toward achievement. Self-assurance is contagious. Even during the most challenging times, a confident leader heightens morale. Confident people inspire confidence in others.

How do you gain confidence and continue to be confident? Belief in yourself comes from within. However, as leadership coach and author Tara Mohr shares, telling yourself to "just be more confident is not the answer."[5] During her *Talks at Google*, she offered a few tactics for how to be sure of our abilities and what we bring to the table. Her tactics include "recognize your inner critic," "unhook from praise and criticism," and "don't wait on confidence."[6]

Although confidence is derived from our inner work, it still comes up against the external barriers that exist concerning pay gaps and promotion opportunities. There are still not enough BIPOC leaders across all industries to represent the multicultural environment that exists. So, when a leader of color gets that seat at the table, looks around, and doesn't see any adequate racial representation in the room, she may question her right to be in that room. Impostor syndrome can arise, leaving her depleted and discouraged. On the other hand, leaders of color have to contend with being perceived as overly confident, which can be interpreted as combative. This is a catch-22 requiring enormous emotional intelligence to navigate.

Let's explore how to take action, whether you feel confident or not. Mohr shares that one of the common reasons women pass on advancement opportunities is because they "didn't feel ready" or they wanted to wait to get more education—assuming that the time between waiting or getting the extra degree was somehow going to instill more confidence. But being confident is about trusting the talents, skills, and gifts you have *right now*, and doing so can often entail gaining a greater awareness of the many things for which you've been thanked and acknowledged. What do you already do really well and feel passionate about? Are you a great teacher? A powerful motivator? You can take a strengths assessment test, such as CliftonStrengths, to help you pinpoint what makes you unique so that you can apply these strengths in all areas of your life.[7] It's also a powerful reminder of the things that make you awesome, which can be a great confidence boost to return to whenever you need it!

X— Insight 3 → o

Lead with Energy and Enthusiasm

Photographer Gordon Parks said, "Enthusiasm is the electricity of life. How do you get it? You act enthusiastic until you make it a habit." Enthusiasm is energy projected from the soul, and it is the conduit to achieving any objective. When it's authentic and not condescending, enthusiasm is infectious.

Why are energy and enthusiasm fundamental to leadership? They help us project an aura of confidence that is beneficial not only to our lives but also to those around us, including the people we lead. As a leader, when you allow enthusiasm to be your pillar, you can help guide teams to optimal productivity. Leaders must seize and maintain their teams' attention while educating them on new objectives and processes, which leads to increased employee engagement. We know that the journey to meeting objectives can be sprinkled with less than ordinary but necessary tasks. An energetic leader can ease the malaise around busy and sometimes not particularly creative work.

The importance of being an exciting, energetic, and enthusiastic leader is not a new concept. However, it is not discussed enough, because some may view the idea as unsustainable and leading to burnout. Michael Hyatt, bestselling author and founder and chairman of Michael Hyatt & Company, has said, "The best leaders don't leave their energy level to chance. They are intentional about creating it." When a leader addresses their team without enthusiasm or energy, the team will not follow. Some team members will leave, taking their innovation and expertise with them. In one of his articles, Hyatt lists some tips (which I have expanded on) for raising your energy.[8]

- **Get a good night's sleep.** Some people need eight hours to feel refreshed and think clearly. Others can feel energized on six hours of sleep. *You* know how many hours you need to feel energetic, so ensure that you get the right amount of sleeping hours you need.
- **Eat smart and healthy.** Again, this requires knowing what your body needs. While certain foods may taste good, they can make us feel sluggish and affect our energy levels—you're probably familiar with the term *food coma*. It is essential to carve out time to eat regularly and healthfully to fuel your body. When you do not prioritize eating, you may be tempted to reach for food that, although convenient, is probably unhealthy.
- **Stay clear of negativity.** People stay in the pits of pessimism because it's an addictive emotion. To consistently project the energy that people want to be around, you must be selective about whom and what you listen to and take in. What may seem harmless on the surface and possibly entertaining, can cloud your mind and impede progress toward creative solutions. We must not underestimate the power of language or the messages we take in on a daily basis.

You don't need to be boisterous or artificial to maintain a

sincerely positive, enthusiastic perspective that comes across in your words, tone, and behavior. You decided to be a leader to positively influence and empower those around you to expand personally and professionally. Just remember, people want to follow and be inspired by those who have a high energy level and are enthusiastic about their work! Let these tips guide you in establishing and maintaining your energetic set point and avoid being a drain on your team due to low energy and enthusiasm.

When you **do the common things in life in an uncommon way**, you will **command the attention of the world**.

—George Washington Carver, educator, scientist, and inventor

CHAPTER 4

Activating the Power of Your Personal Brand

*A*pple. Starbucks. Amazon. What do these companies have in common? If you guessed big companies and even bigger brands, you're absolutely right! Think of the long lines for the newest iPhone iteration, five dollar coffees at Starbucks, and daily packages courtesy of Amazon Prime—these companies with powerful brands have found a way to secure loyalty and a significant following!

Many people would rather leave branding to the big companies, but we can take a few lessons from the Apples and Amazons of the world when it comes to developing our own personal brand.

What is a personal brand? It can be defined as what differentiates you from others. It is your unique value proposition—your strong point. Amazon's founder, Jeff Bezos, says that "your brand is what people say about you when you are not in the room."[1]

In my previous career track, I worked in a male-dominated industry in healthcare system leadership. I was almost always one of the younger executives and usually one of a small handful of Black women who sat at the senior table. Later in my career, through significant reflection and even some feedback about how to create a more powerful brand, I developed more courage when it came to authentically expressing who I was in a variety of ways. I learned that I am much more authentic when I show up as myself, without trying to fit into a box. I like fashion and flair, along with a pop of signature accessories—a beautiful brooch, a silk scarf, or a statement necklace. This is all part of my brand, and I became comfortable and confident in expressing my personality this way, as opposed to conforming to stuffier suited and traditional looks for the workplace.

Here is a practical tool you can use as you think about your own brand. I call it RAIL (an acronym for reflect, ask, identify, leverage).

- **Reflect** on your brand so that you have a meaningful and memorable encounter with every person in every interaction and every time. You want people to remember you and the power of your brand. Take the time to dig deep and be introspective about how you show up.
- **Ask** someone or a few trusted sources around you to share feedback, especially if you don't know what your brand is. Those who know you well can be a good source to help you shape or refine a strong personal brand that leverages your authenticity and strengths.
- **Identify** recurring trends in the feedback. After you weed through the outliers, what are the top trends that keep coming up? (For example, maybe your colleagues or mentors speak recurrently about your honest, direct, conversational style, or about your acumen with technology.) What are your gifts that others recognize that you may not?
- **Leverage** the trends that you heard about from the feedback. What you are best at is where you should focus to create and strengthen your brand. As you start to recognize these themes, consider which of these strengths you can maximize for your brand.

As you think about your brand, always remember that it is based on your reputation, which is a result of your credibility, your results, and how you show up. It results in the *perception* others have and communicate about you even when you are not in their presence. You are in control of that reputation, and it will be key to your career success.

The foundation for that reputation is more than just the effort you put in and the exceptional quality of your work; it begins and ends with your brand. Your brand will be what opens the door for you, and your reputation is what will keep you at the table. Just like the association you make with a logo or company name, others will make similar associations with your work based on the brand you project. Taking time to develop your brand will steer the words in those conversations or on those pages.

When developing your brand, consider what impression you want others to have about you when knowing you or hearing about you. Do you want to be recalled as an authoritative figure or the empathic individual? Do you want to be thought of as the person who is last in the office and first out the door, or as someone who is willing to help a teammate and stay late when needed?

The brand you develop for yourself is the culmination of every action and word you project to others. When assessing your brand, you should also consider both your digital and in-person presence. Let's start with your in-person presence. This is the image you project to everyone you meet personally or who has the ability to observe you in person. This can be carefully choreographed to exude the image you want to portray. Some of the in-person items that impact your brand are:

- your ability to deliver results and convey the value those results bring to others
- your appearance

- your ability to accept critical feedback
- the people with whom you associate
- your tone and verbal communication
- your body language

The first items on the list are determined in the conscious mind; and as you move down the list, they become increasing influenced by the subconscious mind. In other words, you can actively think about and control how you deliver results and your appearance; whereas your tone and body language may be influenced by past experiences, affecting your behavior and actions without your even realizing it, so these items may require more focus and attention on your part.

One definition for branding is "the set of emotions and perceptions that you intentionally cultivate around your business, which you constantly communicate to your customers through a series of visual and verbal cues. Effective branding helps companies or enterprises differentiate themselves from their competitors and build a loyal customer base."[2]

Although this definition applies to businesses, we can reword it to apply to personal branding as follows: Your brand encompasses your emotions and perceptions that you intentionally cultivate around your interactions, which you constantly communicate to your network through a series of visual and verbal cues. Effective branding will help you differentiate yourself from people who have the same skill set so you can build an influential platform.

The same method of branding that applies to physical businesses can also be used for personal branding, which is your bridge to establishing your reputation, ultimately leading to sustained credibility. Developing your personal brand includes building recognition, awareness, and loyalty.[3]

Recognition refers to your relatability as a leader. The people you lead should be able to identify with you. Establishing your brand involves being receptive to new information. When you want to build a positive personal brand, you want to be recognized as someone who seeks out information beyond their purview.

Awareness is the aspect of personal branding that centers emotion as the focus. You are aware that who you are is heavily communicated through verbal cues and consistent behaviors. I want to reemphasize here why self-awareness is so crucial. Suppose you don't know who you are and why you chose to be a leader. In that case, you run the risk of telling a story or sending a message that does not belong to you, which means your behaviors will not be consistent with your message—hence, they will negatively impact your reputation.[4]

Loyalty occurs when your customer or client base prefers what you have to offer over the competition. You don't need to market heavily or convince your audience in order to secure their loyalty. Some facets of brand loyalty include customer trust, satisfaction with what you have to offer, and a demonstrated commitment to coming back to your products or services repeatedly.

For leaders in corporate spaces, it's important to be known for something, as corporate environments are so competitive that having a personal brand will enable you to stand out. Establishing that brand can be even more critical if you are an entrepreneur. However, it's vital to remain true to yourself—never try to be someone you aren't. Instead, view personal branding as an ongoing process to ensure that you are always presenting yourself to your audience in your most authentic form. Give yourself the space to evaluate whether or not values that were once on your list are still valid for you now. Questions such as, "How do I want to grow?"and "Who do I want to become more of?" and "How do I want to enhance my strengths?" can be valuable to you as you continue cultivating a positive personal brand.

Nick Nelson, founder of The BRANDPRENUER Agency®
and a top voice in personal branding and marketing, shared with
me that it's also powerful to ask yourself the kind of questions that
will enable you to build a tenable fan base. These questions include:

- Who are you?
- What do you stand for?
- What's the problem you're solving?
- What's your unique angle to solving that problem?
- How is your way of solving that problem different from
  everybody else's?
- What do people get as a result of engaging with you?

Nelson noted, "You always have to understand that it's not
about you; it's about what's in it for other people!"[5]

Personal brands can be leveraged as a tremendous asset for
those BIPOC leaders in corporate environments. They are the
foundation for how others perceive you, and thus it is important to
do the necessary groundwork to develop your brand.

X— Insight 4 → o

Be a Visionary and Strategic Leader

What exactly does a visionary look like, and why is this important?
As a leader, you need to be able to inspire a compelling vision and
lead your team to achieve goals based on that vision. No one wants
to follow a leader who is unclear about the future or unsettled in
how to drive the organization forward.

Do you have a vision that you can articulate to others? Is it
clear and easy to understand? Is it focused?

Before we address having a vision as a leader within the workplace, let's consider the importance of having one for your own career. This starts with knowing what you want to achieve, or possible dream job titles or companies where you'd like to work. This is the moment where you can be selfish. Do you want to be viewed as an expert in your industry? Do you want to gain more access to public speaking opportunities? Do you want to have more creative freedom? Or do you want to be a strategic thinker and ideate and innovate new lines of business?

Determining what you desire to gain coincides with addressing your reasons for advancing into leadership, whether you want to continue working within an organization, choose to explore opportunities outside your current organization, or go a different route altogether, such as venturing into entrepreneurship. Identifying these reasons will help you establish a framework for the action steps needed to advance and maintain your leadership role.

Being a visionary isn't just about setting your sights on goals you wish to attain; it's about taking others along for the ride so that you have support and buy-in. In his book *The Vision Driven Leader*, Michael Hyatt states that the reason you want to be able to communicate a clear vision to your team is because "your team makes everything else possible."[6] Your goals must be clear and fascinating enough so that you can get your team excited about being an integral part of your vision. Being able to communicate a specific destination to your team also enhances each member's autonomy and confidence.

Coupled with being a visionary leader, you must also be a strategic leader, which requires thinking beyond your operational and business unit. In other words, having a long-term action plan that helps you steer your decisions and eliminate any options that don't concur with the bigger picture. A strategic leader understands the need to accommodate for unpredictability and anticipate new industry innovations.

To be strategic means to think critically, and this mindset leads to effective complex problem-solving. There's no doubt that as a leader, you face countless challenges. Being strategic eliminates the temptation to be reactive rather than proactive. A reactive response neglects the ultimate objective by omitting the need to address whether a particular action corresponds with the vision. A reactive response is a lazy way to tackle a problem. A strategic leader is proactive by choosing intentional actions. Arnaud Chevallier's Strategic Thinking in Complex Problem Solving presents an interesting four-step process for problem-solving that keeps a leader in strategic mode: framing, diagnosing, potential solutions search, and implementation.[7]

Let's look at this four-step process using the challenge of talent retention as an example. Using Chevallier's approach, we first frame the problem by acknowledging that talented employees are leaving the organization. In the diagnosing step, we identify the reason this is happening. For instance, employees are leaving due to lack of advancement opportunities. Next, we would search for potential solutions that address the root of the problem before we move into implementation.

In our example, even though the need for new employees is immediate, a strategic leader won't just hire for the sake of getting bodies in seats. They will be more apt to hire for the overall future of their department and the company. Working with a strategic mindset means you understand the element of balance; that is, you exercise patience and train your eye on the long view while recognizing that some decisions have to be made within a given timeframe—and it requires a firm, confident, capable leader to do just that.

x—Insight 5 → o

Build Your Thought Leadership Internally and Externally

What is a thought leader? I'd like to share the perfect description Denise Brosseau offers in her book *Ready to Be a Thought Leader? How to Increase Your Influence, Impact, and Success*: A thought leader is "someone who can move and inspire others with your innovative ideas, turn those ideas into reality, and then create a dedicated group of friends, fans, and followers to help you replicate and scale those ideas into sustainable change."[8]

The following names come to mind when I consider influential and effective thought leaders:

- Daymond John is the CEO and founder of FUBU (For Us, By Us). Known for his marketing prowess, he is an entrepreneur, investor, and a highly sought-after speaker and consultant. He is also an author of four bestselling books and has been a longtime host on the show *Shark Tank*.
- Mellody Hobson is the CEO of Ariel Investments and serves as chairman of the board of trustees of the Ariel Investment Trust, the company's publicly traded mutual funds. Outside of Ariel, Hobson is a nationally recognized voice on financial literacy and made history as the first African American woman to join ownership ranks of an NFL team.
- Bozoma Saint John is a longtime marketing executive who made history in June 2020 when she was hired as Netflix's chief marketing officer, making her the first Black C-suite executive at the company. Saint John is an outspoken

advocate for greater diversity and inclusion in the C-suite and beyond and has used her platform to call on more companies to do more than pay lip service when it comes to diversifying their workforce.

- Sylvia Ann Hewlett, CEO of Hewlett Consulting Partners and founder of the Center for Talent Innovation, is known for her thought leadership on gender issues in the workplace as well as sponsorship for career success. She "has the distinction of being the most published author ever in the *Harvard Business Review* (17 articles and counting)" and "has written 16 critically acclaimed books."[9]
- Johnny C. Taylor, Jr., president and CEO of the Society for Human Resource Management, is a global leader on the future of employment, culture, and leadership, and a highly respected voice on all matters affecting work, workers, and the workplace.
- Arianna Huffington, author, philanthropist, and businesswoman, is perhaps best known as the co-founder of the *Huffington Post*, a news aggregator and blog. She is also the founder of Thrive Global, a company that was created to focus on vital health and wellness information.
- Harriet A. Washington is a medical ethicist and considered the foremost authority on the concept of the medical maltreatment of Black people. She is the author of several books, including the 2007 National Book Critics Circle award–winning *Medical Apartheid: The Dark History of Medical Experimentation on Black Americans from Colonial Times to the Present*.

Keeping these exemplars in mind, let's explore why you should be a thought leader. Building your thought leadership will bring you and your organization significant credibility. Think about the last conference you attended: the main stage speakers, the breakout sessions, and other sessions during the event. The speakers who were on stage were there because they are thought leaders, and they were sought out to share their expertise with a broader audience. Even if they had submitted a proposal to speak rather than being invited, they would not have been approved for a speaker's stage unless the event organizers felt they had significant expertise to offer.

Thought leaders increase trust and establish a reputation that travels far beyond perception. Consistently offering your expertise across various platforms can make the difference between consumers choosing you, your product, and your service over your competitor's. It can also be the difference between an organization choosing you for certain high-level roles, or choosing someone else instead.

I spoke with Carol Cox, founder and CEO of Speaking Your Brand®, a coaching and training company that helps high-performing, purpose-driven women entrepreneurs and professionals create their signature talks. Through her company and content, her mission is to empower more women to find and use their voice, to tell the stories that need to be told, and to activate ideas for change. We had a conversation about thought leadership, and why it is so valuable. She said, "When it comes to thought leadership, you can take it with you. It's not specifically tied to that job, to that company, or current organization. Within your job role and company, you're going to have accomplishments and achievements; however, they are closely connected to that specific organization—whereas your thought leadership is not owned by your company. They are your ideas, which are portable."[10]

You will achieve a strong sense of personal accomplishment when you can finally own the fact that you have expertise that your organization needs—and that can be harnessed beyond it. Whether you are in consumer goods, manufacturing, health care, fintech, or any other industry, your goal as a thought leader is to establish yourself as a subject-matter expert and then become known for it.

Let's talk about what being a subject-matter expert means. It entails being the one whom others in your organization come to consistently when they have a question or a problem that needs solving. Some may think it arrogant to call yourself a subject-matter expert or thought leader—and I will caution that we all need to have a high degree of self-awareness about our skills and also leverage what we do best—however, it is not arrogant or selfish to acknowledge your *expertise*.

Remember, in building your brand, you *always* want to be known for something—whether that is being an exceptional public speaker, an expert in customer service, or a LinkedIn influencer. Whatever you are known for should be specific and speak to your expertise. You want to showcase what you know and give others a reason to be your "fan," as they will advocate for you in meetings and for opportunities you may not even be aware exist. So much of what you do as a leader is building trust, relationships, and influence, all in an effort to drive results in your organization. Being seen as a subject-matter expert and thought leader gives you significant influence inside your organization.

Now, let's also look outside your organization or workplace. Usually, being active in your community or in professional societies or volunteer organizations is a plus and can present an opportunity for you to build thought leadership. Think about where you support various causes or utilize your leadership skills. As you broaden your scope outside the workplace, you can consciously start to showcase your capabilities and subject-matter expertise. The more people start to see and hear you, the more relevant you will become.

Aside from professional benefits, being a thought leader offers increased personal expansion. You will become increasingly confident in what you do, which will lead you to explore other avenues that align with your expertise, allowing you to reach and connect with even more people. Invitations into circles you may not have had access to before will appear. For example, your expertise can move you into other industries you might never have considered in the past.

People are attracted to people who attract people! Read that again. Being a thought leader increases your influence, and your number-one goal is to influence; that extends to your boss, your peers, your direct report or teams, and even those you may not work with regularly.

Let's merge our knowledge of why we need to be thought leaders with how we nurture and maintain the qualities of being one. Hopefully, you are leading, or will lead, in arenas that focus on subjects that matter the most to you. To lead with authenticity, you need to be known for something you feel passionate about. Although there are distinct steps to becoming a thought leader, you will find that it is not always a linear process. You may often find yourself completing all steps simultaneously, then repeating each step at an elevated level. Let's look at the process.

- **Introduce your point of view.** You have to find a way to confidently introduce your concepts to convey your ideas in the most effective way, since you are opening yourself up to scrutiny. Remember, as a visionary leader, it's your job to present a compelling vision.
- **As you introduce what you know, you can then add to your sphere of expertise.** You can start by sharing what you excel at in a particular industry. As you add to your sphere, you can present how your expertise can be employed in other sectors. Expanding your sphere in this manner will assist you in developing a goal to make your message more palpable.

- **Once your message becomes more palpable, you can create new approaches to communicate your expertise with others.** No matter what you do, though, you must be consistent in your practice. Consistency helps you remain true to your message while establishing very clear ideas.
- **Continue to do an internal check.** What does this mean? Stay self-aware! This keeps your goal of becoming a thought leader pure; remember, the goal is always to inspire and empower.

Although accolades and awards can result from effective leadership, being a thought leader has more to do with influence and the positive impact you have on others. There is a massive amount of responsibility and opportunity when you step into the role of a leader, since more and more people will come to you for advice. If you are serious about building your thought leadership (and you need to be serious about this!), consider ways you can share your expertise broadly outside of your organization to bring you even greater credibility inside of your organization. Ask yourself the following questions:

1. *What do I want to be known for?* Spend time reflecting on your capabilities and your passions, as well as how you can leverage them to become a subject-matter expert and thought leader.
2. *How can I get my expertise into the world and share my thought leadership, both within and outside my organization?* Use some of the guidance in this chapter to brainstorm and to get yourself out there!

Carol Cox also shared a handy acronym with me that is useful in applying to your own thought leadership: VOICE.

- **V**—Have an interesting *viewpoint* for your topic that's unique in your area of expertise. Cox says, "Think about it this way: What's something that needs to be talked about more within your industry or circle of influence?"
- **O**—Be *open*, bold, and direct in your communication. Cox shares, "You're not afraid to share opinions. . . . That's the only way that people will start to recognize you as a thought leader."
- **I**—Share your *individual story* so that you universalize it for your audience, giving examples of how something has personally impacted you. Cox says, "As experts, we stick to the facts and have the answers. A thought leader says, 'I'm going to take this expertise and integrate myself into it.' It's my personal journey, my emotions, that create that human connection with my audience."
- **C**—Have a *container* or a project for your thought-leadership message. For instance, your container could be a book, a podcast that you create, a LinkedIn live show, an event that you host, or an initiative that you are advancing.
- **E**—Be *emotive*, real, and vulnerable with your content and your delivery. Cox notes, "It's bringing the emotions and feelings into what it is you're talking about, because that is what will resonate so much more with your audience, and it's going to make your thought leadership that much more memorable. Think of it in terms of having an asset that is completely yours. . . . Women and men of color have a lot more challenges within corporate because of unconscious bias, conscious bias, favoritism, and the like. In being a thought leader and stepping up and sharing

those ideas consistently, you can't help but be noticed."[11]

x– *Insight 6* → o

Develop Executive Presence and Image

One of the things I remember from my childhood is the amount of time it took my mother to get ready to go anywhere. Whether it was the drugstore, Walmart, work—you name it, it took time. She took great care in ensuring that she always presented herself well when she left the house. Even a quick run to the local grocery store was a task in getting ready. For family gatherings, it was a frequent joke that you had to give my mother enough time to prepare to get to the event—regardless of what it was!

Due to my mother's influence, I liked to dress nicely wherever I went. In high school, I was voted "best dressed" during my senior year. In college, before my classmates and I went to do our administrative internships, we were required to take a professional-development course in which, to ensure success, we were encouraged to "show up our best" on our first day and beyond. Our professor shared that we should always be prepared to be judged when we walked into a room, and that we needed to step it up and "look the part," like we belonged in the administrative offices and other spaces within the healthcare organizations where our class was interning that summer.

None of this was really news to me; it simply reaffirmed what I always knew. It was drilled into me at an early age that you don't leave the house looking "any kind of way." I had always dressed to feel like I belonged. My younger self believed that if I looked nice, I would always be accepted.

After I graduated from college and before I embarked on my

master's degree, a mentor told me, "Dress for the job you want, not the job you have." This always stuck with me; I took it to mean that I needed to ensure I was always one step ahead, and I could do this through my attire. From suits and heels to tasteful accessories, as I started to climb the corporate ladder, "looking the part" took on a whole new meaning for me.

Certainly, looking and dressing the part and ensuring you have an elevated appearance are important aspects of developing a commanding executive presence that causes others to take note. However, appearance is only one—albeit critical—part of executive presence. In *Executive Presence: The Missing Link Between Merit and Success*, Sylvia Ann Hewlett describes executive presence as a combination of how a person acts (gravitas), speaks (communication), and looks (appearance).[12] Hewlett also notes that nobody attains a top job, lands an extraordinary deal, or develops a significant following without this combination of confidence, poise, and authenticity that convinces the rest of us we're in the presence of someone who's the real deal.

Clearly, executive presence is more than just image; it also encompasses confidence, which we explored in the last chapter. When someone exudes executive presence, they have the kind of confidence and gravitas that show others that they belong.

Hewlett also wrote an article, "Cracking the Code That Stalls People of Color," that notes:

> According to new CTI research, [executive presence] constitutes 26% of what senior leaders say it takes to get the next promotion. Yet because senior leaders are overwhelmingly Caucasian, professionals of color (African American, Asian, and Hispanic individuals) find themselves at an immediate disadvantage in trying to look, sound, and act like a leader. And the feedback that might help them do so is markedly absent at all levels of management.[13]

Considering executive presence may not be something easily

accorded to BIPOC leaders, it's important for all of us to consider the following questions:

- In white male–dominated environments, who makes "the rules" on what executive presence is and whether someone does or does not have it?
- When it comes to what is considered professional and unprofessional in terms of executive presence, how are natural hair, braids, or dreadlocks viewed?

Many BIPOC leaders feel pressure to conform to the standard-issue dress code in a predominantly white workplace, and they are also aware of an existing double standard that places extra emphasis on people of color falling in line with expectations. A Black male, emerging executive shared with me that he works in a very conservative organization where the dress code "is black, white, blue, and gray, and you almost have to fit in that. . . . I feel like I can never dress down because I will be judged. It's almost like I am in an environment where if others wear a polo for casual Friday, then I have to wear a polo *and* a sports coat—and I definitely don't feel safe enough to show up like everyone else. Even when others can show up on a Zoom call at home with a T-shirt on, I would never get to pull that off without a side eye or a few side eyes."

For multicultural women especially, our "crowns" are sacred ground and off-limits, yet we continue to be embroiled in conversations about whether our hair fits the mold of professionalism. It is absurd that we are even discussing whether or not it's possible to have executive presence if our hair does not conform to standards set by whiteness. The CROWN (Create a Respectful and Open World for Natural Hair) Act was created in 2019 by the personal-care brand Dove and the CROWN Coalition in partnership with then-senator Holly J. Mitchell of California. The purpose of this legislation was to ensure "protection against discrimination based on race-based hairstyles by extending statutory protection to hair texture and protective styles such as braids, locs, twists, and knots in the workplace and public schools."[14] The Dove CROWN research study revealed that Black women are 1.5 times more likely to be sent home from work because of their hair. It also showed that 80 percent of Black women surveyed felt pressure to change their hair in order to fit in at work.[15]

A Black female healthcare executive shared a story with me that may likely resonate with you. "I got an internal promotion at the company where I was working, and it required me to relocate to a major metropolitan area. At the time of my promotion, I was wearing my hair in braids. However, I decided that I instead wanted to wear my hair in its natural state, with twists. It was neat and nice, or so I thought. Everyone loved my hair; however, I could tell that my new CEO wasn't particularly fond of my hairstyle because of her reaction the first time she saw my hair styled in that way. Because of this encounter, I reached out to a mentor to ask her opinion about whether I should keep the hairstyle or change it. After a few conversations, she encouraged me to change the style, and went further to say, 'You don't want to die on the sword for your hair. When you arrive [meaning once you have made it to a certain level career-wise], then you can wear your hair however you want, and no one will ask questions at that point.' So, I asked, 'When do I know that I have arrived?' She answered, 'All you need to know is that you're not there yet.' Shortly thereafter, I added in a hair weave. When I got to work that following Monday, my boss, who had initially grimaced at my previous style, commented how much she loved my hair and said specifically, 'You should keep it like that.' Mind you, she never once commented about my hair previously when it was in short twists. I felt like I was letting down myself and others by not standing up for something like my hair, especially when I liked the way it was."

There is a happy ending to her story, however. Fast-forward more than ten years, and she was up for another promotion. Here she was, contemplating her hairstyle again, and specifically its cultural and political impact in this new and very visible executive role. Fortunately, "I had a totally different conversation with my then leader who honestly didn't understand the importance of the hair topic." At that point, my friend decided to call the same mentor from years ago, and the conversation ended with, "'You've arrived, so wear your hair like you want!'" She shared with me that for the first time in her executive career, she felt like she could be her authentic self!

This story was so emotionally gripping for me as a Black woman. I can detail countless examples of other Black women who have also encountered negative comments or reactions about their hair in their workplace.

As men and women of color, *we should never have to choose between cultural authenticity and executive presence.* Granted, most people of color in the corporate world understand the reality of "paying our dues" in order to get to where we can exercise greater agency in dress and the like. Clearly, societal perceptions that put BIPOC leaders at a disadvantage are likely to place a greater burden on us to change who we are in order to conform with preexisting expectations. At the same time, if we move beyond physical appearance, it becomes clear that executive presence is often about the perception that you have what it takes to be a good leader or solid executive.

The following table highlights the traits that can either enhance or detract your executive presence.

Strengths	Weaknesses
High energy	Low energy
Enthusiastic	Bored and disinterested
Sincere	Insincere
Prepared	Unprepared and unaware
Clear and concise communications	Rambling and babbling
Warm and approachable demeanor	Aloof, cold, and distant
Dynamic personality	Uninteresting and uninviting
Confident and charismatic	Lacks confidence
Polished and pulled together appearance	Disheveled and unkempt
Natural and relaxed	Fidgety and nervous
Emotionally intelligent	Lacks emotional intelligence
Strong posture	Slumped over
Uses vocal variety	Flat voice with no inflection
Compassionate	Unkind or unsympathetic
Positive body language	Unwelcoming or cold body language
Looks the part	Too casual for the role
Self-confident	Too critical or overly self-deprecating
Articulate	Poor word choice or overuse of slang and jargon

If your executive presence is an area where you think you need some improvement, I have outlined some items to consider.

- What is your mindset? Executive presence is more than how people perceive you and starts with how you perceive yourself and your skill set. Eliminating self-doubt and enhancing your own self-confidence is the foundation for a strong executive presence.
- Have you asked for feedback? As with your personal brand assessment, seeking input from people you trust to share their transparent thoughts about your presence, image, and overall persona can help you understand where you may have blind spots and room to improve.
- How adept are you at managing your emotions? When you receive bad news, do you fly off the handle, or are you calm yet firm and direct with your questions? (We'll go into more detail about emotional management in the next chapter.)
- Are you as confident as you can be? Your ability to exude confidence about your subject matter and in delivering messages to your team is crucial to having executive presence.

Remember, executive presence is a very subjective yet critically important trait whether you are already in a leadership role or are aspiring to advance to one. You don't want to put yourself out of the running for opportunities due to your lack of executive presence. As a leader of color, having a high degree of executive presence is critical to your success in corporate environments.

"The most **common way** people **give up their power** is by **thinking they don't have any**.

—Alice Walker, author

CHAPTER 5

Utilizing Your Social and Emotional Intelligence

The term *emotional intelligence* (or EQ—emotional quotient —when it refers to the testing measurement of someone's emotional intelligence) was first used in 1990 by researchers Peter Salovey and John Mayer, and can be described as the ability to perceive and manage emotions in ourselves and in other people.[1] Emotional intelligence has since entered our cultural lexicon as a valuable "skill," but it's so much more than a couple of buzzwords. Why is it so important when it comes to developing yourself as a leader? Having finely developed emotional intelligence is a critical component of who you are, what you do, and most importantly, how others perceive you.

According to studies done by psychologist Daniel Goleman, who popularized emotional intelligence with his bestselling book by the same name, emotional intelligence has been found to be twice as important as performance with respect to technical skills and IQ (intelligence quotient). This applies to jobs at all levels.[2] Goleman furthered his research by comparing those he labeled "star performers" to "average ones in senior leadership positions." He found that nearly 90 percent of the difference in their profiles was attributable to emotional intelligence factors rather than cognitive abilities."[3] Goleman's studies suggest that emotional intelligence is more critical to business success than one's intelligence level.

Goleman noted five critical elements that make up emotional intelligence.

1. **Self-awareness**—This entails having a clear picture of your strengths and weaknesses, as well as an awareness of how your emotional states and the things you express might be impacting others.
2. **Motivation**—Motivated leaders have a high standard of excellence and constantly pursue activities that will lead them closer to their goals. They also tend to be optimistic and inquisitive, finding the glass "half-full" rather than nitpicking on why something can't be done.
3. **Empathy**—With empathy, a great leader has the capacity to put themselves in another person's shoes, building rapport and team cohesion, while also being able to compassionately challenge others and offer constructive feedback when needed.
4. **Social skills**—A leader with good social skills can effectively communicate, resolve conflict, and gain the support of their team members.
5. **Self-regulation**—A self-regulated leader knows how to keep their emotions in check and be fair in their assessments and treatment of others. They take time to reflect on their emotions and thoughts without making rash decisions or compromising their values.

An emerging executive shared with me the power of learning to manage his emotions. "Because I tend to be very expressive, I was encouraged to think about how my reactions and body language come across to others in meetings. I also think about the conversations I had about the struggle of being in certain environments yet being the one who could rise above the stress in meetings and being able to motivate and encourage the team to move toward execution."

Together, the five dimensions of emotional intelligence tell an important story. Experts agree that approximately 90 percent of companies will use EQ testing for potential employees, particularly executives. EQ tests are now used by approximately 82 percent of global companies for executive positions; 72 percent of these companies use the tests for middle management; and 59 percent of companies use the tests for entry-level positions.[4] TalentSmartEQ, a provider of emotional intelligence training and development, tested emotional intelligence alongside thirty-three other important workplace skills and discovered that EQ was the best predictor of performance, accounting for 58 percent of success across all job types.[5]

If there's any doubt about the bottom-line importance of a high EQ, just consider the case of a Motorola manufacturing plant where 93 percent of employees became more productive after the facility adopted stress-reduction and emotional-intelligence programs. Another factory reduced "lost time" accidents, boosted productivity, and sharply lowered formal grievances after supervisors received training in emotional competencies.[6]

While there are varying components of emotional intelligence (and some experts have argued that EQ doesn't adequately translate to communities of color that might have slightly different social mores and ways of communicating compared to white-dominant corporate spaces), this chapter's insights focus on different ways of approaching the five main elements that Goleman identified—and putting them to good use, in a way that promotes greater connection and understanding. Moreover, there is growing evidence that EQ is helpful in a mixed work environment that includes both white people and people of color. In a survey, nearly 60 percent of founder respondents said that in years shaped by the pandemic and a racial-justice crisis, incorporating EQ into organizational culture is more important than ever.[7]

Recognizing the importance of exercising EQ, as an effective leader it's paramount to build a concrete understanding of how your emotional states impact you and the people around you. When you learn to navigate your emotions skillfully, you will have a better chance of maintaining balance in the midst of heated situations and understanding others, to the extent that you'll relate to them with greater ease and facility.

x— Insight 7 → o

Know Who You Are—And How Others See You

Let's start with Goleman's first element of emotional intelligence: self-awareness. What this really comes down to is your capacity to accurately assess yourself and know who you are as a person and a leader. What are your strengths and capabilities? What might your blind spots be? It's not enough to see yourself with as much accuracy as possible; it's important to be clear about how you receive feedback from others and how they perceive you.

As a leader, you must be willing to assess yourself regularly. That may seem obvious at this point, but it deserves mentioning again. It's only truly possible to know yourself when you are able to examine yourself as you are, not as you think you should be. This is not an easy process, because when done with sincerity, unknown biases, fears, and insecurities can rise to the surface. Knowing yourself is not a destination either; it is part of the journey, so having a support system to sustain you is vital. As underlying beliefs are revealed, identifying and processing your feelings with the help of others around you can dismantle the expectation of perfection that's often placed on leaders.

Let me give you an example of self-knowledge that poses as self-awareness but really isn't. We've all heard a leader or entrepreneur proclaiming, "I'm a control freak," or "It's hard for me to delegate." Let's be blunt here: Although this person appears to indicate they know themselves well; most likely, those comments were made at a time when the person was *not* fully aware of themselves, their vision, or their abilities. If they had been, they would be willing to question the efficacy of their behavior. Instead of saying, "This is just the way I am," they would be capable of determining whether this is something that helps or hinders them, as well as how it impacts others.

When knowing yourself and your impact on others becomes just as important as brushing your teeth, you are no longer going to make these types of dead-end observations about yourself. Instead, you become clear about your strengths and weaknesses in a way that invites celebration as well as change (if it is needed). With respect to the example I offered, not only will you know *how* to delegate, but you will also be more than ready to commission those functions that align more with the strengths of your team members! In short, exercising self-knowledge and self-assessment also expands your ability to read others, to understand how they are relating with you, and to establish rapport. Counterintuitively, it's the opposite of "self-involved." When you are able to see yourself clearly, you get a handle on the bigger picture and learn to extend that thoughtfulness to the people around you.

x– Insight 8 → o

Be Intellectually Curious

Goleman noted that motivation is one of the most important facets of emotional intelligence. As I've discovered, a capacity for curiosity is a powerful part of sustaining motivation. As author Ruth Burke wryly noted, "Only boring people get bored."

We all have the ability to look at things around us and either be stimulated or not. A lack of stimulation can indicate you might not be perceiving things as fully or in as engaged a manner as possible. Being curious is strongly tied to active listening, which we'll dive into in a little bit. When a leader shows strong interest in their employees, it makes people feel secure, especially when a leader actually takes action on the feedback they receive. But of course, a leader can only take in what they value, so developing intellectual curiosity is all about learning to expand your attention to include things that may not necessarily appeal to you or capture your interest at first glance.

As a leader, it is particularly important to be deeply engaged with what is happening externally and internally. Moreover, remaining curious keeps you mentally flexible and agile. It leads to the ability to ask more and better questions. Asking thoughtful and carefully crafted questions demonstrates your ability to think critically about what you are hearing. Being intellectually curious in meetings, for example, shows your ability to hear information or data points and reflects in such a way that your questions are a representation of how you are synthesizing what is presented. Showing intellectual curiosity is the act of staying in a mental state that values inquiry and can help you continue to grow, rather than getting trapped in what you already know (which includes your expertise in a given area).

X- Insight 9 → o

Understand Others on Their Own Terms

In concrete terms, Goleman defines empathy as one of the most important hallmarks of emotional intelligence. It seems like a no-brainer, right? If we were to survey leaders with the question, "Are you empathetic?" the results would likely yield a 100 percent yes response. Let's dig into that question a bit more deeply.

Are you a good listener? How do you react to ideas that differ from your own? Do people feel comfortable approaching you with negative news? If someone has ever said to you, "I didn't want to tell you because I was afraid of how you would react," it is a sign that you are not as empathetic as you thought you were and it indicates that you may have some difficulty getting out of your own head and understanding others on their own terms. Luckily, it's possible to develop empathy, as well as any of the other facets of emotional intelligence.

Empathy is something lots of people don't understand. They think it means feeling sorry for someone or, sometimes, even condoning bad or erratic behavior. That isn't the case. Empathy is a genuine understanding of a person's feelings. So often, we are limited by our own perspectives, which we then use to judge or relate to other people. To be empathetic, instead of staying stuck in the box of our own opinions and life experiences, we make a genuine effort to recognize and acknowledge that other people might be coming from a completely different perspective. Instead of being defensive or judgmental, we can use active listening and compassion to build rapport by understanding and appreciating another person's perspective.

Why is this so important? The ability to see things from other people's viewpoint is strongly connected to cultural competence. Regardless of the industry you work in, the structures, the processes, and the way business is done are constantly changing because of globalization. Being culturally competent has always been vital to the success and sustainability of any corporation. With the recent shifts in global consciousness, consumers are demanding that organizations be more responsible in ensuring cultural inclusivity and making the workplace safe for people to express their full identities. A true leader knows that there is "a complex, organized, and dynamic system of learned beliefs, attitudes, and opinions that each person holds to be true about his or her personal experience."[8] This approach is so valuable because it seeks to understand people on their own terms and honor different ways of being as well as the unique perspectives offered by these differences.

Furthermore, we can't talk about understanding others without discussing compassion. The word *compassion* comes from the Latin *compassionem*, which literally translates as "to suffer together." Emotion researchers associate it with the feeling that comes up when we are motivated to alleviate someone else's suffering. While empathy is about the ability to put ourselves in someone else's shoes, compassion relates to the desire to offer help to others based on what they need. Let's focus on compassion in the context of a leader's role in helping team members advance.

Here's a simple example: You become aware of a department leadership role in which one of your team members would excel. You have been privileged to witness this person's steps to gain the qualifications and confidence necessary to fulfill the role. You present the opportunity to her, but instead of excitement, she begins to list all the reasons she is not ready. Since you have already established rapport with her, you recognize her self-limiting beliefs. As you address them with her, you realize that the limiting beliefs have surfaced from her childhood experiences—as is the case for most of us. With compassion—not pity, which entails feeling sorry for someone, thus placing them in a disempowered position—you approach this team member. As a compassionate leader, you actively listen to offer support in a way that is appropriate for that individual's growth. I use the word *appropriate* because not everyone benefits from the same type of support; this is another reason building relationships and exercising emotional intelligence to determine what's needed is so vital.

There's a common assumption that "business is business," and employees should leave their problems at home. But as complex human beings, it isn't always easy (or even desirable) to compartmentalize our experiences. Our lives impact the work we do, and the work we do (as well as the environment we are doing it in) has a demonstrable effect on our personal life. A compassionate leader understands and welcomes their team members' humanity.

During these current times, in which remote work has increased beyond our wildest expectations, the need for compassion is more pronounced than ever before. Many people are experiencing new stresses, including isolation and the uncertainty that comes from navigating expectations in the time of COVID-19. Mastering the art of human connection through understanding must be our primary focus. Leaders and organizations have been forced to recognize that we are not just worker bees or machines equipped for constant productivity; we are integrated human beings with rich emotional lives, needs, and gifts that should be responsibly resourced and nurtured. Leaders must consider the complexities that remote working has added to how we collaborate and perceive each other. Since connection has proven to be crucial for companies to progress and actively compete in the marketplace, leaders must become more intentional and creative when it comes to genuine networking that values the whole person.

Good leaders are laser focused on their team members' growth and expansion. They demonstrate this in their approach to providing feedback and during discussions about appraisal, salary increase, and promotion. These are the kind of leaders who naturally draw greater support and commitment from their team members. When employees know their leaders care about them—not just their work but also their entire well-being—the result is almost always increased loyalty and the sense that we're all in this together.

x— Insight 10 → o

Communicate Impactfully and Listen Actively

Let's look at Goleman's fourth dimension of emotional intelligence: social intelligence. Adele Lynn calls social intelligence "social expertness" in her book *The EQ Difference*. She describes social expertness as "the ability to build genuine relationships and bonds and to express caring, concern, and conflict in healthy ways." [9]

Let's explore how this looks in practice. How do people react when they see you walking down the corridor? Do people look forward to speaking with you? Much like empathy, your social intelligence (SI) is measured by your ability to listen to, consider, and ponder ideas that are different from yours. However, your SI level is also based on your willingness to collaborate and how you view conflict. An effective leader does not approach conflict negatively. You understand that through conflict, innovation can arise, and new ways of approaching challenges can become the new standard. SI also involves accepting when someone's idea is more appropriate than yours and not taking it to mean that you aren't good at developing solid ideas.

Overall, SI can be summed up, practically, as great communication skills, both verbal and nonverbal. Communication isn't just about what you say; it's also about how you are communicating through things like your tone, voice, and actions. In addition, communication isn't a one-way street. It encompasses active listening and the capacity to exercise the kind of patience that allows you to carefully observe others before speaking. Just as an empathic leader is keen to the surroundings that encompass the experiences people bring with them, SI is a leader's continual invitation for their team to share ideas and regularly initiate meaningful discussion of goals and overarching vision. In being impactful communicators, we develop our teams to build similar skills.

As we all know, communication skills are a critical factor when it comes to high performance. Impactful communication goes beyond talking, making yourself heard, or getting your point across. In her book *Talk Less, Say More*, Connie Dieken offers the following guidelines: "Get to the point, be specific, focus on the person, and avoid a one-size-fits-all pattern."[10]

Let's break down these tips even further. *Getting to the point* forces you to be succinct and communicate with clarity. This is especially instrumental in presenting a vision to your team. It can also be advantageous during emergencies, when time is of the essence. Consider the COVID-19 pandemic. The crisis prompted healthcare professionals like Dr. Shlomo Noskow, an emergency-room physician who described long hours in the hospital filled with "constant damage control," to invest more time in communication training.[11]

Now, let's look at what it means to be *specific*. This coincides with getting to the point. Because you are speaking concisely, you offer clarity to your audience. Being specific can prompt meaningful dialogue within teams, which can provide an avenue for moving into new thoughts and ideas. Specificity also ensures that others know exactly what you are talking about, and are not mired in ambiguity or trying to guess what you mean.

Next, let's examine what it means to *focus on the person*. I'm not sure when it began to occur with greater frequency, but today, interruptions during conversations have become the norm. When you have not allowed a person to complete their thought, you have listened only long enough to respond, not to understand. While it takes practice, being intentional about becoming a better listener (which I'll talk about in just a bit) demonstrates a desire to build connections. Being focused on the person shows that you are eager to listen to their ideas, which will also make them more receptive to hearing you out—making it a win-win for everyone involved.

Finally, what does it mean to *avoid a one-size-fits-all pattern*? Everyone has different perceptions, and we bring all our varying impressions to conversations both in and out of the workplace. As a leader, you are likely already aware of these differences, since you have developed a rapport with your team members. This tool is especially useful when you need to provide feedback on performance. Whether the input is to congratulate someone on a job well done or to give feedback on areas that require immediate improvement, you will know how to relay the information in a meaningful way for that person.

Remember, communication isn't just about what you say, it's also about how you take in both nonverbal and verbal information. Have you ever heard the phrase, "Two ears and one mouth means listening is twice as important as speaking"? To that end, you must integrate active listening into your daily leadership.

Active listening is powerful in many ways. For one thing, it creates an atmosphere that makes people feel comfortable enough to ask questions that lead to increased understanding without the

feeling of being judged for requesting clarification. The continual
mastery of active listening can also help leaders proceed with strategic planning. As Michael Hoppe writes in his book, *Active Listening:
Improve Your Ability to Listen and Lead*, "Leaders benefit from the
depth of engagement and information that can come as a result; it
lets them plan and proceed with greater insight and knowledge."[12]
Imagine strategic planning taking less time and perhaps, dare I say,
becoming easier because your awareness has expanded to new levels
due to active listening.

In her book *Speaking As a Leader*, Judith Humphrey offers
ways to listen more efficiently. Humphrey identifies three different
levels of active listening that are important to consider.[13]

1. **Physical**—This level of active listening focuses on visibility. As a leader, regular communication with your team
   and peers is not optional. Physically, you display your
   capacity to listen by offering cues through your body
   language, such as nodding, making eye contact, and
   ensuring that you are physically tuned in.
2. **Mental**—Humphrey suggests that leaders ask themselves
   the following questions before they address their team,
   peers, or audience: What is my audience thinking about
   the topic I will address? and How can I move *my audience from point* A *to point* B *mentally?* This level of listening entails paying attention to what a person is saying in
   that moment. For example, if an audience member has
   reached a conclusion about your presentation that you
   were not expecting, ask how they arrived at that. Listening at the mental level begins even before a meeting or
   presentation. It starts with those daily interactions we
   take for granted, like the informal, unplanned "jam sessions" where a conversation on any topic ensues between

two people, and others gather casually to join.

3. **Emotional**—Humphrey makes an excellent point that illustrates how listening at the emotional level can make conversation about a severe matter less uncomfortable. Part of our responsibility as leaders is to guide people through complex circumstances that derive from within the organization or from team members' personal lives. When people communicate, they use certain words for a reason. There is a meaning to every word, and the purpose may not have anything to do with the situation at hand. At this level, listening with heart comes into play to ascertain what is at the crux of one's message. (It's also a great way to define one of the traits of empathy.)

Let's look at an example of how all these different levels of listening work. You are in a productive session with your team for the purpose of setting milestones for a project. Each team member takes their time to speak about their personal responsibility for the project's success in order to display their understanding of their role. You are pleased with the excitement and assurance that everyone demonstrates as they verbalize their responsibilities. Through observation, you notice a team member affirming his role with words; however, his body language and tone display something different (*physical*). It could seem easy for you to observe his body language as a sign of fatigue. However, you do not want to dismiss this discrepancy. What could appear as a minute issue may cause a disastrous domino effect on the entire project.

So you choose to address this team member privately and ask him some questions about what he's experiencing (*mental*). As you approach him with your observation, you find that, in fact, he is very excited about his role in the project. However, he just learned that a loved one received a disappointing medical diagnosis.

This example displays how crucial active listening is; it is just as much for another's benefit as it is for yours. You would have missed out on an opportunity to show you care not just about his career advancement or even the project, but that you also care about his well-being (*emotional*). Overall, active listening takes us beyond merely observing what's on the surface and into the realm of the unspoken.

As you might expect, exercising active listening doesn't only help us to establish rapport with our team members—it also leads us to make decisions that we might not have otherwise considered. A Black male senior executive I spoke with recalled having many conversations with his staff about managing the hospital where he was incident commander during the early days of the COVID-19 pandemic. The hospital was closing units, restricting access to the facility, and making drastic changes to the visitor policy, among many other operational tasks. He recalls that in one of the many meetings where they had to make critical staffing and service-level decisions, certain areas of the cafeteria had to be closed, including the popular grill station.

"The conversation ensued about wait times, long lines . . . and then one of the leaders spoke up and said, 'How much more are we going to cut?'" he recalled. "And I quickly was able to see that this wasn't just about closing the grill station. After a little while longer, I said, 'Everyone get some fresh air and we'll meet back in thirty minutes to continue the conversation.' I then followed the leader who had spoken up out of the room and asked her what was going on because I could sense that this wasn't just about the grill. She burst into tears and basically said her staff was overwhelmed, and some of them had seen more death in the last eight months than they had seen in their career. And for some people, the only sense of normalcy was to go down to the cafeteria and get a cheeseburger. At that moment, it was my emotional intelligence that led me to hear her and be empathetic. We got back to the room and I said, 'We're not closing the grill—we need to figure out a way to spread people out and be more efficient.' That was just one of the many topics where we had to figure it out, but I stress that my emotional intelligence allowed me to read from her and dig deeper to figure out what was happening. Had I been tough, who knows what the response could have been? But as a leader, I have to make tough calls, and sometimes, the tough calls will go against the grain when you are using EQ skills to help you navigate what seem like small decisions but in essence have big impacts, especially in times of duress."

Thinking about and paying attention to *all* the levels of listening can lead to incremental improvements in our communication skills. Ultimately, the goal is to listen in order to improve our interactions with everyone around us as well as the outcomes we might experience. Being honest about where we can improve our communication is not the same as judging ourselves; it enables us to realize opportunities for more growth and enhanced relationships.

If you're looking to enhance a single skill to amplify your emotional intelligence, my advice is to begin with *how* you communicate. Countless resources are available that can assist anyone at any career level to become a master communicator. The one resource I'd like to highlight here is the organization Toastmasters International, where individuals around the world have utilized tools to improve their communication and leadership skills in a supportive environment. Although Toastmasters focuses on public speaking, the personal and professional development skills one gains by being an active member go far beyond communications alone.

x— Insight 11 → o

Leave Your Ego at the Door

Finally, let's look at Goleman's fifth dimension of emotional intelligence: *self-regulation*, which picks up on self-awareness. While the latter enables us to see ourselves and our impact more clearly, the former enables us to monitor and manage our emotions, thoughts, and behaviors in ways that produce positive results for us and the people around us. When we are self-regulated, rather than acting on impulse, we deal with our stressors so that we can sustain focus and connect with others more effectively.

I chose to focus this insight on the value of leaving your ego at the door because it's a crucial component of self-regulation. When individuals have not matured in emotional intelligence, they might engage in selfish and aggressive behavior to get what they feel entitled to. Phrases like "There he goes again, throwing his weight around!" describe this kind of self-involved behavior, which points to an inability to understand and manage one's emotions. The consequence is that such a person ends up acting in harmful ways they might not even be conscious of.

This behavior is sometimes evident in the decision-making process, when leaders unfairly use their position of authority to manipulate others. In these cases, the decisions are not made to improve the team's success or enhance the knowledge of team members; they are made to make the leader look good, or simply because the leader can make them. If the decision results in an error, we can expect this leader will not own it and will most likely blame the team.

This is not how an influential leader makes decisions or interfaces with their team!

Some leaders think being decisive involves ego-based action. Making decisions consists of delegating, designating who will take specific responsibilities, and gaining feedback from your team. Once a decision is made, the leader allows the team to apply their genius to the objective and ensures that everyone has all the resources they need to bring the decision into full effect. A strong leader examines the root causes of problematic situations to find solutions with a sense of calm and ease and takes ownership over all decisions that are made.

What do I mean when I talk about the *ego*? It is the *I* or the *self* that feels, thinks, and expresses. When taken to an extreme, it can be the self-importance and self-interest an individual uses to react to their external environment.[14] While psychologists describe multiple levels of the ego, the ego, in and of itself, is neutral. However, it can become unbalanced; for example, when it is overinflated or deflated.

You must realize that as you rise in your career, more people will become familiar with you and want to know you. With an inflated ego, you can develop an unhealthy affinity toward power, status, and popularity. An ego-focused leader is authoritarian, meaning their management style gives them complete decision-making control and power over subordinates. Such a leader makes decisions with little to no feedback from others. While there might be a time or place for such a leadership style, it is largely detrimental to trust and loyalty. With an authoritarian leader, team progress is hindered because the leader has no interest in encouraging and influencing.[15]

These may seem like extreme examples, but at some point, we've all experienced an inflated ego, which is why self-regulation is so important! You can determine whether you need to reel in your ego by how you behave in a conversation: Are you preparing to speak and get your point across without actively listening to the person talking? Are you gearing up for an argument, without having received creative input from everyone involved?

Let's look at some early warning signs that your ego is becoming inflated.

- **You compare yourself to others.** You may be inspired by someone you know because they have reached a level of career success that you desire. You start to compare yourself in a way that causes you to forget there are many ways to get to a destination. You forget that personal experiences influence how an individual progresses.
- **You are defensive.** Often, defensiveness comes from a sense of having to protect ourselves and maintain ownership over our ideas. We all want to celebrate the times we produce a new idea, but we cannot make the idea our identity. Being overly invested in a view will hinder us from accepting that another idea could be better.
- **You don't allow others to showcase their own brilliance.** As a leader, you must be able to take a step back and allow others to speak about their accomplishments.

The ego can also be deflated, which leads to low self-esteem, a lack of confidence, and the inability to be assertive and ask for what we need. A deflated ego also translates into constantly seeking acceptance, approval, and validation from others rather than developing a genuine conviction in one's own ideas and qualities. When a person has a deflated ego, their confidence is based solely on feedback from other people, and they feel adequate only when someone tells them they did a good job. On the surface, this might look like cooperation or collaboration, but it isn't. When a leader has sufficient self-confidence, they tend to be more relaxed, flexible, and easier to communicate with. They also inspire confidence in others.

Neither a deflated or inflated ego is good for leadership. A healthy ego is necessary to lead people. The ego can help you become stronger in a particular circumstance by reminding you of your skill and talent to overcome a challenge that seems impossible. Getting out of balance can happen to anyone, but we can maintain an egoic balance with patience and self-regulation. We can keep our ego in check and ensure that we are coming into our interactions with a sense of fairness and the intention of making solid connections with others.

Trust yourself.
Think for yourself. **Act** for
yourself. **Speak** for yourself.
Be yourself. Imitation is suicide.

—Marva Collins, teacher, founder of the Westside Preparatory School in
Chicago, Illinois

CHAPTER 6

Leading with Authenticity

*H*ow do others see you? Do they know your values, perhaps even without you having to announce them? Who are you? Are you consistent in your personality? Do you change how you communicate based on who you are working with at any given time? Do your morals and values shift when you are around certain people?

If you've practiced building emotional intelligence, you've probably already asked yourself these questions. The more committed you are to answering these types of inquiries regularly, the more knowledge you will have of who you are; therefore, the more authentic you can be. Through authenticity, as a leader, you can connect and share with others while still maintaining appropriate boundaries. A compelling leader understands authenticity is a priority in building relationships within a team. However, an internal clash can occur when trying to maintain authenticity while also preserving privacy and boundaries. Being an authentic leader isn't about revealing every last aspect of your personal and professional life to others; it is about being relatable and approachable and placing a premium on the relational aspect of leadership, which is what helps you build meaningful connections with the people around you.

The pressure we may feel to be authentic—performing as our

"true selves"—can be alleviated when we recognize that every single person is much too complex to be pigeonholed into one specific persona. In truth, part of being a self-aware leader (going back to emotional intelligence) is featuring parts of your character and personality that reveal what is most important to you. An important part of authenticity—beyond the fact that it gives people a strong sense of who you are and goes a long way in building rapport—involves communicating your genuine values with those you lead. This helps others gain insight into how those values influence your decisions. When others see that you are consistent in what you say, what you do, and how you act, you establish trust and inspire morale with greater ease because you've demonstrated that you have integrity and are not the kind of leader to be swayed anywhere the wind blows.

When team members are dedicated to a vision, they also desire to connect with their leaders. Authentic leaders can readily create a connection with those they lead, which creates an environment conducive to career growth. The team will view their leader as a trusted advocate for their advancement. Relationships with leadership also influence how team members interact with each other. If a leader shows no interest in sharing their values or shows up as a different person every day, this behavior affects how the team functions. It also hinders initiation and does little to invite collaboration.

If being authentic is such an important aspect of leadership, why is it so difficult for many leaders to find and express their authenticity? Perhaps this is because the environments we choose to be in can impact how we express ourselves. In her book *The Art of Authenticity*, Karissa Thacker encourages leaders to seek "a good cultural fit [where] you can focus, learn, and develop aspects of yourself as a leader."[1]

Here, it's important to note that questions of authenticity

fluctuate with how people are perceived by their societies. So many BIPOC leaders, Black ones in particular, go to work each day, feeling they have to pretend to be someone they're not for hours on end (a phenomenon known as code-switching, which we'll talk about in greater depth in a bit). It is exhausting—and over the course of one's career, it is draining and depleting. It culminates in hiding ourselves, our emotions, our thoughts, and our comments to avoid being stereotyped. More specifically, it can also look like changing the inflection of our voices so people will not think less of our intelligence, wearing certain clothes to fit in, or worrying whether our faux locs or natural hair will be perceived as being unprofessional. Through my own in-depth conversations with Black leaders, I have come to understand that many of us go through our careers with the extra burden of educating others about our blackness, our culture, and our respective backgrounds.

Every single person deserves to be perceived in a way that is free from the distortions of bias, stereotypes, and misconceptions about who we are and what we are capable of. Unfortunately, many leaders of color have discovered that their individual accomplishments and qualities are juxtaposed against the discriminatory lenses through which others see us. Thus, we often find ourselves trying to present ourselves—our speech, behavior, and even facial expressions—in ways that combat stereotypes. This is known as *impression management*. While it is certainly a skill that many leaders have learned to master, it takes an additional emotional toll on those of us who might be burdened by the pressure to be seen as "acceptable" or "deserving" of our position, especially if we are the only leader or person of color in our work environment.

x— Insight 12 → o

Understand Code-Switching

Our conversation about authenticity would be incomplete without an insight on *code-switching*, which can be defined as the "ability of a person to switch between languages or dialects to meet communication needs. It is also the alteration of clothes, hairstyles, and music from one environment to another to be accepted."[2]

Code-switching is essentially changing how you express yourself to fit into an environment where there is a certain strict standard of expression. There are many costs to code-switching, especially among people of color. The *Harvard Business Review*'s Big Idea Series on Advancing Black Leaders notes that code-switching is meant to "optimize the comfort of others in exchange for fair treatment, quality service, and employment opportunities."[3]

Research suggests that code-switching:

> often occurs in spaces where negative stereotypes of black people run counter to what are considered "appropriate" behaviors and norms for a specific environment. For example, research conducted in schools suggests that black students selectively code-switch between standard English in the classroom and African-American Vernacular English (AAVE) with their peers, which elevates their social standing with each intended audience. We also see examples of guidelines encouraging black people to code-switch to survive police interactions, such as "acting polite and respectful when stopped" and "avoiding running even if you are afraid."[4]

So many of us have been taught to believe that, in order to be successful, we have to code-switch or otherwise shrink ourselves. BIPOC—especially Black leaders—are more likely than their peers of other races to say they have felt the need to, and absolutely had to, code-switch in order to "fit in." For so many Black leaders, code-switching is a familiar practice and has even been a survival tool for us in corporate America.

One of my interviewees, a Black male senior vice president in the insurance industry, recognizes that leaders of color, accustomed to feeling restrained or unwelcome at the table, have "somehow muted our true selves to align with, be accepted in, and assimilated into corporate environments." He noted that this experience has been a constant for him over the past two decades, working in a role where he has global responsibility. While he mentioned that there seems to be greater freedom to explore topics related to race since the murder of George Floyd in 2020, "I still don't feel like I have earned the right to bring my authentic self to work. Early on, we were taught: this is how you dress, this is what's expected, this is what you have to look like in a corporate role. I felt that I had to ask myself: What am I willing to sacrifice to be able to be a part of this organization? The industry that I started out in is notoriously very traditional and conservative. The look was blue suits and white shirts with a tie. To show my personality, perhaps I could wear socks that were a little funky but that was the extent of expressing my authentic self in the workplace."

An emerging healthcare executive, also a Black man, shared similar experiences and expressed that he feels pressure to compartmentalize his life, revealing himself only in spurts. "For example, when there is something fun happening or a team retreat, I am usually the one my colleagues turn to for the entertainment because they want my energy or my voice to help drive the fun aspects of the meeting. However, I also want people to see that I am exceptional when it comes to data analytics and the operations side, too, and that I have just as much to contribute in those areas as I do with entertaining at meetings. . . . I feel like, if I were a member of a country club, I could easily talk about that with my peers, but to bring in other aspects of who I am, I definitely leave those in a box, and the box doesn't get opened at work."

Some might suggest that code-switching is standard for all of us, based on whether we are in a formal or informal setting. Many of us would not talk to our grandparents the same way we would speak to our friends; or perhaps we'd behave differently at work from how we would during a vacation or happy hour. These are indeed examples of code-switching because we are changing our language, gestures, and how we speak based on our environment. However, for the purpose of this book, we are taking the concept of code-switching beyond general or simplistic terms and addressing how it impacts professionals of color. Although some people might argue that code-switching is a "superpower" that can help people navigate varied spaces, research suggests that Black leaders in particular experience code-switching as a phenomenon that comes at a cost and disables them from truly being themselves in the workplace. When a BIPOC leader code-switches, she changes all aspects of herself, from how she dresses to how she speaks, to prove that she belongs in the boardroom with the rest of the executives. Her communication is employed for the purpose of continuously proving herself against negative stereotypes, and this takes a toll over time.

Chandra Arthur is the founder and CEO of several businesses in the technology sector. Her TEDxOrlando talk discusses code-switching and its adverse impacts on authenticity and diversity. Arthur begins her brief speech by sharing that her choice to be a leader in the technology space was to "change the world in a positive way." [5] Often, women of color feel pressured to behave in an appropriate, scripted manner instead of allowing their authenticity and spontaneity to shine through. As Arthur shares her experience of attempting to obtain venture capital for her businesses, she notes that "women of color receive 0.2 percent of venture capital in the tech space."[6] She goes on to share that she believes deliberate code-switching allowed her access into certain spaces she would not have had otherwise had she been unwilling to come across as "culturally compatible." She had to be a "non-threatening person of color" in order to find acceptance in a predominantly white space and receive its advantages.[7]

Black social innovation, excellence, and entrepreneurship are nothing new, but for decades, Black professionals have used code-switching to facilitate navigating spaces and environments where white people have been the majority. The practice has been known to assist Black people to thrive in the midst of racism and discrimination, by diluting their perceived blackness to make others feel comfortable.

Often, the question raised in conversations about code-switching has been: Should people of color, particularly Black people, continue to code-switch or not? It is evident, through many of the dismal statistics about leaders of color, that code-switching has not been enough to help people of color move beyond the barriers of systemic racism. Placing the onus on any one individual to amend their behavior in order to cater to systems put in place by white culture is, quite plainly, wrong and even offensive. Softening one's vocal inflections, adjusting a handshake, and conforming to standards set by the dominant culture will not be enough to displace racist systems.

At the time of his TEDx talk at Iowa State University, Justin Roberson was beginning his PhD studies in higher education administration. During his speech, he shares his experience of being the recipient of professors' biases, and how it felt to be surrounded by people who saw him through the lens of stereotypes rather than respecting his individuality. Roberson suggests that instead of code-switching, a code break must occur, and he offers three methods he believes would successfully initiate such a code break. He says he would have given these three methods to his professors during his undergraduate career to alleviate the pressure on him to code-switch in order to be recognized, heard, taken seriously, and valued.

1. **Check for shared meaning in a story.** Roberson urges listeners to receive clarification when an individual is sharing an experience. Receiving clarification eliminates the temptation to make assumptions.
2. **Affirm the story.** This allows the storyteller to be the expert in their account. Some people believe they fully understand specific experiences because of their closeness to other cultures and backgrounds. Affirming one's story shows a level of respect for that person's individuality.
3. **Be comfortable with non-closure.** When listening to another's experience, you may not receive understanding immediately. It would be best to be receptive to the possibility of having several conversations before closure is obtained. [8]

Roberson's three methods are remarkable because they place the onus of code-breaking not on BIPOC, who are already dealing with the heavy emotional labor of code-switching, but on those who are connecting with BIPOC and who might be unaware of how their implicit biases could be guiding the conversation and robbing people of color of their full identities. People of color understandably employ code-switching due to subtle and overt pressure from dominant white culture to behave in ways that deny their full humanity. In order for us to be free from this, we must recognize that it's up to the people around us to alleviate some of that pressure by doing away with the biases they might be placing on another person's humanity.

Leading is already challenging enough; when you combine

leading with deciding between what behavior is "culturally compatible" versus authentic, this can take a toll on a leader's vision and energy. All industries and organizations need to realize that developing an environment conducive to embracing cultural differences adds undeniable value to any business.

x— Insight 13 → o

Be Vulnerable

An important component of authenticity is *vulnerability*. Sociologist Brené Brown, in her book *Daring Greatly*, describes vulnerability as "uncertainty, risk, and emotional exposure."[9] Vulnerability can make us feel shaky, like we are stepping out of our comfort zone or relinquishing complete control, but it's so important because it establishes our humanity and makes us more relatable to others.

Vulnerability is a characteristic that, when used appropriately and meaningfully, can be a powerful tool to build relationships and connections with others. As a leader who embraces vulnerability, you reveal that you are courageous enough to share your learning and life moments.

Our life includes the career and the leadership roles we play, the organizations we are a part of, as well as a combination of our relationships outside the workplace. As leaders, we can only have an impact when we make genuine connections with others: those we lead directly and indirectly, those we work with as peers across the organization, those we report to, and other key stakeholders.

Being vulnerable fosters increased connection with your team, which can lead to improved professional relationships. Your connection with people outweighs the act of simply sharing a story. When you are willing to be more open—to the extent that you can share your so-called weaknesses or even laugh at yourself a little —it encourages team members to make a connection, which can improve individual and team performance.

Of course, as I've mentioned earlier in this chapter, one of the keys to being vulnerable and authentic is a clear recognition of boundaries and how and when to share, in addition to understanding that what you share vulnerably should add value to the person or the situation at hand. Unfortunately, this is where people make the mistake of oversharing. To establish a balance, it is vital to ask yourself, "Is sharing this story appropriate for the moment?"

When being vulnerable, it's also crucial to practice self-regulation. (I'll be coming back to the power of emotional intelligence over and over!) A healthy and balanced approach to vulnerability means you know when you need to stay silent for a moment before offering a suggestion or sharing a decision. Moreover, if you need to make a decision but are simply not in the right mental space to do so, an appropriate display of vulnerability would be to note transparently that you need more time, but would not necessarily entail giving your team members a litany of reasons why.

Expressing vulnerability appears in small yet significant interactions. Leaders make the mistake of believing that being vulnerable involves large gestures or occurs during momentous situations, but this isn't necessarily true. In the end, give some thought to how you can be vulnerable, and do it with intentionality and appropriateness to the situation at hand.

x— Insight 14 → o

Build Trust Early

We know that trust is cultivated between people through authentic interactions and consistent behavior. This gives way to trust that is earned and then reciprocated. Typically, it does not matter who initiates the trust, but when you choose to step into a leadership role, you have essentially raised your hand to say, "I will be the one to initiate the continual flow of trust."

Let's look at several ways a leader initiates and cultivates trust within their team. As we've already discussed, vulnerability builds connection, and it also goes a long way in building trust. It's easy to share sentiments of fulfillment and happiness when everything is going well. However, when a leader shows vulnerability by sharing feelings of confusion and even concern during times of change or uncertainty, team members will appreciate that honest expression because they are reminded that leaders are human, which in turn can help to build trust within the team.

A leader also builds trust by having intentional discussions with their team to offer their reasoning behind a specific action. As a leader, when you share your reasoning behind a decision, you create space for your team to understand and ask questions for clarity. This kind of transparency goes a long way. Additionally, focus on how you are supporting your team with the tools and resources they need to succeed to drive results for the organization. By taking these steps consistently, you are building trust with your team by demonstrating that you are a supportive leader who advocates for them when the time calls for it.

"You don't make progress by standing on the sidelines, whimpering and complaining. **You make progress by implementing ideas**.

—Shirley Chisholm, politician and educator

CHAPTER 7

Strengthening Your Decision-Making Skills and Embracing Change

*B*y now, I hope it's obvious that, while there are many different ways to be a leader and embrace your unique skill set as such, there are certain qualities that will only serve to enhance your growth if you do the work to cultivate them. Decision-making is one of those qualities, and it's an absolute nonnegotiable if you want to convey the kind of authority that will make people want to trust and follow you. Good leadership requires the ability to make firm, intelligent decisions, sometimes on a dime and without a guarantee that anything will work out. Just as there is no one definitive type of leader, there is also no one way to strengthen your decision-making abilities. This process requires both logic and intuition—and of course, it also depends on the specific situation at hand. Decision-making is a multidimensional process that requires collecting sufficient information and carefully weighing your options while simultaneously holding a willingness to forge ahead when time is of the essence. It is one of the most important responsibilities of a leader. For BIPOC leaders who may be dealing with challenging interpersonal issues in the workplace, decision-making is instrumental to your ability to command respect and influence others.

Of course, one thing that can test our ability to make strong and swift decisions is when we are in a transitional period. For example, the COVID-19 pandemic essentially threw "certainty" out the window and put leaders in a position where they were called upon to make rapid decisions without additional information or even the hope of receiving information down the line. This requires resiliency (which we'll be diving into in greater depth later in the book) and involves taking ownership and expecting your team to do the same by helping them to step into their genius. If they are already in the practice of doing this, although you may not have all the information you need to make the decision, you and your team can still take action with confidence. Your decision-making skills will make all the difference and inspire others to harness their strengths to the best of their ability!

Let's stay on the topic of the pandemic, and how it changed the course of business and our lives in such a way to enjoin leaders to make decisions that would further impact their teams. In the midst of the pandemic, we saw international demonstrations fueled by pleas for the end of racial injustice everywhere. Increased division and tension existed in almost every aspect of daily life. The theme of uncertainty and unsettlement existed inside and outside organizations; this even applied to fully remote companies in 2020 and beyond. Leaders had to take into account the chaotic environment that surrounded them and steer their teams through often-turbulent waters.

Cathy Hughes, the founder of the largest African American–owned broadcast network, Urban One, offered some insight in an NPR interview. She shared ways she used resilience to lead during the drastic changes ensuing from the pandemic. She expressed that even though there were decisions that had to be made immediately, she advised to allow "yourself as a leader time to think about what it is going to take to overcome."[1] As urgent as the times may be, being resilient does not involve rushing to see how much can be done before things get worse!

Hughes shared that she had to furlough 382 broadcasters and decrease salaries across the leadership team, including her own, by 20 percent to avoid additional layoffs. She also tapped into her resilience by being optimistic (leading with energy and enthusiasm—Insight 3) and acknowledged her own fear (being vulnerable— Insight 13). Hughes's actions demonstrate that being a strong and resilient decision-maker is not about ignoring present realities; it involves a careful balance of optimism and doing what is necessary. Although Hughes acknowledged her level of concern, she focused on the opportunities that come from extreme change and uncertainty.[2]

Change and uncertainty are not always accompanied by detrimental consequences, as we have seen in the pandemic. Change can bring about innovation that perhaps was not apparent before the disruption occurred. For instance, Janice Bryant Howroyd, founder and CEO of ActOne Group, a workforce solutions organization, experienced many changes after opening her first office in Hollywood, California, in 1978. While having no contacts, no clients, and no recruits, she stayed focused on how the uncertainty that loomed over her business would open the doors to new opportunities she could utilize to grow it. After being open for some time, Howroyd described the tension that arose for her company around pricing against competitors. She began hunting for "over the shelf" technology that would fit what she needed, but she could not find anything suitable. She realized that time was of the essence. Instead of allowing frustration to derail her, she remained receptive to the idea of creating her own technology solutions. She decided to gather a team of developers to build what she coined "human-friendly technology."[3]

Uncertainty provides avenues for leaders and companies to experiment. It can lead to the discovery of a higher-capacity level that may not have been apparent previously. Disruption can lead to the acceptance of new business models. For example, businesses that never considered selling their products or services online found success in building web-based stores during the pandemic.

Even on a personal level, unforeseen changes can bring about new ways of viewing your career. If you have been static, change can provide necessary variety for advancement. You can use uncertain times to assess what you are doing as a business, or business unit, and find an opportunity to affect more people positively. We learn to make some of the most important decisions of our lives when we use uncertainty as an opportunity to enhance an organization's mission. As a leader, when you accept change as a learning experiment, you can also make decisions that enable you to examine your responsibilities, as well as whom and what you are committing to. This is where the rubber meets the road, and you can determine whether you have been living up to your title or if there is more to do.

x— Insight 15 → o

Recognize and Work with Ambiguity

Piggybacking off the topic of uncertainty, an effective leader is someone who learns the importance of operating in the face of *ambiguity*, "something that is not clear because it has more than one possible meaning."[4]

If you are in an ambiguous situation, it may be difficult to determine your plan and steps to achieve your goals. Role and task ambiguity are the two common areas where leaders or employees may experience a lack of clarity in the workplace—which, of course, can make it extra challenging to make effective decisions.

Perhaps the most frustrating career and leadership experience I have had was when I was in a role that was not only unclear to me, but also to countless other leaders I was tasked to work with (and they said so)! This led to anxiety and disengagement, and I felt a constant lack of confidence in my own abilities, although many empathized that I was in a challenging role that lacked a bigger strategic picture.

It's also difficult to work on a project with an unclear goal, timeline, scope, or attendant resources. Of course, it is clearly much easier to drive results and manage projects when you have all the necessary details.

I realize I have addressed the criticality of various leadership competencies in such a way that they all seem to be the most important if you want to advance your career and have significant leadership success in the corporate environment. However, the capacity to operate with ambiguity is often what sets a leader apart from the rest of the crowd. There will be times when you will not have all the information or data points you need to make a decision. Whether you are missing one piece of data or many parts of the story at hand, it is critical to have confidence in your skills and abilities to make the tough calls regardless. You need to be able to trust yourself, come what may.

Equally important is the idea of being able to "see around corners." In other words, you must be proactive enough to consider all the alternatives and implications of a decision. The higher you go in leadership, the more important it is to be able to have a 30,000-foot view of projects and decisions, and to anticipate the ramifications of your decisions. Mitigating potential fallout is just one of the many opportunities you have to flex your leadership muscle. Remember, your ability to deal with adversity is a huge part of what will define you as a leader.

As I ascended higher in the organizations I worked within,

I became comfortable with not having every single detail, while still remaining nimble and open enough to make informed decisions based on the data I had at the time. Nor did I allow the absence of information to throw me into a state of paralysis and indecision.

Team members need leaders who are willing to take a strong stance and make a clear and firm decision. However, a lack of information should not lead you toward reckless decisions that come from a place of desperation! Remember to take a deep breath and check in with your gut as well as the hard-won expertise you've accumulated over the years.

I also advise you to keep the following three strategies in mind, as they will help you navigate ambiguity and see around corners.

- **Manage your emotions and maintain your composure—always!** No matter what the situation, maintaining your composure is key, because others are always looking to you for cues on how they should react. When you are faced with ambiguity, approach the situation calmly and know that you can control only what you can control.
- **Always have a plan A, B, C, and D!** I am sure you have heard of this adage, and it holds true—especially when you may have made a decision to go one way, but the initial lack of information leads you in a different direction. Proper damage control entails planning ahead for all possible outcomes and contingencies.
- **Communicate, communicate, and communicate more and often.** In ambiguous situations, keep an open line of communication with your team to lessen their anxiety. Leaders can often forget that many people are impacted by their decisions, so if you have the opportunity to alleviate stress and worry–and dispel rumors—take it! After all, lack of information can create tension, and your role

as a leader is to lessen those tensions so people can excel in their work.

x— Insight 16 → o

Be a Change Leader

In a world that is constantly evolving, it's paramount to strengthen your decision-making skills, and this brings us to the topic of change management. As the world becomes more globalized, processes and ways of conducting business are rapidly transforming. Leaders must provide solid guidance so they and their teams can adjust quickly to swift and dramatic change in processes, department mergers or eliminations, and roles and responsibilities.

While change can sometimes be scary, the truth is that most people and organizations thrive on it, especially when they focus on retaining talented people whose gifts are optimized and properly utilized. As an example, the Walt Disney Company has established Disney University to provide guidance to employees when it comes to workplace change. The University promotes organizational values called the Four Circumstances: innovation, organizational support, education, and entertain.[5] These values rely on a leader's ability to guide employees through transformation (change) by encouraging their development in engaging and memorable ways, offering an exciting environment to retain talent, and using empowering language that places an emphasis on everyone succeeding. For example, a change leader inspires employees to pursue opportunities to advance their technological skills. A change leader will also ensure that employees have the resources to leverage advanced technology.

An effective change leader must also understand that when

an organization is implementing change, they have to stay abreast of all the reasons for that change. This is connected to the power of developing a clear, coherent vision that team members can get behind, which we discussed in chapter 4. Sometimes, these reasons get lost in the shuffle, and the focus becomes on the logistics of managing the change rather than why it's crucial in the first place. This also brings us back to the power of a clear and strategic action plan (Insight 4) that carefully denotes exactly what will change and how. Change management is also all about execution. A leader who can manage change knows that execution is one of the most important things they will want to be known for. From my experience, successful leaders focus on ensuring that the right people are in the right positions to execute for change and monitor progress along the way (more about that in the next chapter). In contrast, unsuccessful leaders get bogged down in micromanaging.

It's crucial to consider that for an organization to evolve successfully, there must be a fine balance between change and stability. In other words, according to the Center for Creative Leadership, this can be seen not as a problem to solve, but rather, as a polarity to manage. To help your organization achieve its full potential, acknowledge both poles simultaneously.[6]

x— Insight 17 → o

Lead Hybrid Workforces Effectively

Hybrid workforces and remote work are not a new concept. Well before the pandemic, some companies already understood that their overall vision was more essential than employee location. In the last two years, even companies that had vowed never to offer remote work as an option have been forced to reconsider; now, these companies are actively searching for people who desire remote work.

At the beginning of the pandemic, many companies adopted the phrase "when things go back to normal." Let's be honest here: many organizations were saying this, hoping they would not be forced into innovative solutions for keeping employees engaged and offering alternative ways to work. However, new ways of working have unfolded that no longer allow companies to be lackadaisical about engaging their employees more directly. More and more companies have amended their old-school approach and created a hybrid workforce: either all employees split their time between working from home and coming into the office for meetings, or some employees work at the office while others work from home a majority of the time.

What has this meant for leadership? Leaders must continue to develop ways to keep teams interacting with each other virtually in creative and meaningful ways. Leadership teams must stay abreast of the technology they need to adopt to ensure that employees have the necessary resources to work remotely in a productive way. For change leaders, this also involves advocating for employees to receive enhanced and ergonomically safe home-office equipment, for example. These factors cannot be ignored; if one company is not actively taking care of employees, you can guarantee that many other companies are implementing methods to retain high performers and attract even more.

With the growth in the remote and hybrid workforce, another factor comes into play. As a leader, you must collaborate with employees to create healthy boundaries around being online versus off-line. Employees must be encouraged to unplug. Even though it has always been vital, balancing and prioritizing emotional well-being has become an even more important factor, given that home- and work-life are so heavily integrated (more about that in a later chapter). The pandemic has uncovered the disappointing truth that encouraging this balance for employees has not been a priority for many corporations.

As the work-from-home movement took flight during the early days of the COVID-19 quarantine, many, if not most, people in the workplace faced similar challenges, navigating health and safety concerns, worrying about job security, and wading through the emotional struggles that were the result of increased isolation. These challenges were especially exacerbated for some segments of the population. Women and leaders of color were having the "hardest time, both in the workplace and balancing work and home life."[7] For example, when exploring work-life balance, women are more concerned than men about the upkeep of household chores. Because women feel pressure to keep up with home responsibilities and still assume a disproportionate bulk of household chores, they face greater concerns around the possibility of their careers stalling. According to a McKinsey report, 73 percent of women place concern on household responsibilities versus 65 percent of men.[8]

Between 2015 and 2019, there was a noticeable, albeit slow, rise in the number of women in leadership roles in corporate America. As of 2020, that progress stalled. As more and more companies allowed employees to work from home, women felt and still feel greater pressure to work more hours. As companies have set dates for employees to return to the office full-time, career advancement among women, who already feel the pressure of stretched time and responsibilities, may suffer. With respect to the issue of burnout, which is a huge concern that has received greater attention during the pandemic, 75 percent of working women show concern for those challenges versus 69 percent of men.[9]

While some companies have gone entirely remote indefinitely, the companies that have required employees to return to the office have faced resistance from employees, which has been an unprecedented impetus for organizations to extend the work-from-home arrangement. This is especially important in considering that COVID-19 unearthed biases in the workplace that have been present but were routinely ignored and dismissed as a made-up fallacy or attributed to the imaginations of the underrepresented. The pandemic forced companies to either continue with their plans around establishing an organizational culture that values and pri- oritizes diversity—or to *actually* implement a strategy. Among the companies that are still struggling to create a diverse environment, leaders of color are not rushing to return to the office. Because of the slow movement toward inclusivity among many organizations, they are missing out on a vital opportunity for progress. Courtney McCluney, a professor at Cornell University, stated, "This was the first year that I haven't had my hair commented on and touched without permission in my professional life. . . . I actually like not having to go into the office and be constantly reminded that I'm the only Black woman there."[10]

This is by no means a purely anecdotal experience. Accord- ing to a Slack Future Forum survey, "a whopping 97 percent of Black respondents in the US said they preferred a fully remote or hybrid workplace. Only 3 percent of Black workers surveyed said they wanted to return fully in person, compared with 21 percent of white workers." Another survey from Slack showed Black work- ers expressing a "50 percent increase in their sense of workplace belonging and a 64 percent increase in their ability to manage stress once they began working *from home*."[11]

While people generally enjoy the flexibility of alternating between being in the office a few days a week and working remotely, Black professionals face a heightened ambivalence around return- ing to the office. They have reported that, since working remotely, they have felt an increased sense of ease as they recognize they can be themselves in ways that may not have been possible in the office environment. For example, for Black professionals, working remotely has curtailed the pressure to pretend to be unaffected by reports of racial injustice or news of yet another police killing of a Black or Brown person.[12]

Let's look at some practices that leaders can engage in to address concerns related to workplace flexibility—particularly among other BIPOC professionals.

- **Advocate for their team's choice to return to work.** This will require time to analyze whether a return to the office is necessary by asking whether the need to be in the office immensely impacts company operations or is a tactic for maintaining some semblance of normalcy, or even control over employees. It's important for leaders to recognize that a remote or hybrid workforce does not necessarily impact the efficacy of the business. Leaders must remain receptive to new images of how a so-called typical work environment can look.

- **Advocate for a solid plan to return to the office.** This plan can be developed when it's determined that certain work responsibilities genuinely require an office presence. The plan will need to include supportive measures for the team so that the transition from home back to the office is gradual and easeful. A gradual move can alleviate stress and leave space for professionals to complete projects and begin anew once they return to the office. This time can also allow leaders and professionals to maintain the hybrid setup as a constant option.

- **Initiate regular virtual networking events.** For example, a corporation I previously worked for hosted end-of-day happy hours at headquarters. The event was a convenient way for departments to intermingle without the hassle of leaving the workplace to meet at a different location. This same company also dedicated an area of headquarters to showcase the employees' artwork. These same events can be translated into a virtual environment, but will require a commitment to creativity on the part of leaders. It does not matter what form the event takes; the purpose is to ensure that teams do not lose their connectivity.

- **Recognize team members for their contributions.** Leaders cannot ignore the value of sharing their teams' accomplishments. They might have dedicated time to share the team's achievements in the office, but this time may need to be adjusted during remote work.

- **Ensure that career-advancement plans launched among team members do not lose momentum.** Leaders can initiate meetings that ensure remote work doesn't stall career advancement for the professionals on their teams. This will ensure that a plan previously set in motion is still in effect and will uncover any necessary adjustments to accommodate for changes during the process of remote or hybrid work. Even as we flow through change in the workplace, both small and large, we can continue to keep our eyes on the prize and ensure that everyone in our midst feels supported in building careers they love and can take genuine pride in.

Good leaders must know how to reward those who succeed and know when to retrain, move, or fire ineffective staff.

—General Colin Powell, first African American secretary of state

CHAPTER 8

Creating and Sustaining a Culture of Accountability

*I*t's impossible to talk about change management without stressing the power and importance of creating and sustaining a culture of accountability within your organization. In a nutshell, *accountability* is acknowledging that you, and you alone, are responsible for your actions and decisions. These decisions might encompass the completion of assignments in a timely manner and a methodical, transparent approach to making decisions. Being accountable is not just an idea; it's a lifestyle. Of course, as a leader, placing your attention on your ultimate objective is crucial. It is also necessary to address with your team how you will go about concretely achieving your intended goals.

Structures of accountability should not be punitive in nature, but they should include consequences for poor performance or errors that have larger ramifications for the organizational culture and business at large. But again, the focus should not be on holding your team accountable out of fear that they might be punished; it should be on rewarding excellence and transparency and encouraging team members to learn from their mistakes. Achieving department and company objectives takes on a more significant meaning when people can take pride and ownership in the actions and decisions they took to meet those objectives—and when they are continuously held to the high standards they may have set for themselves. Healthy accountability not only furthers your organization's bottom line, but it also creates an environment in which people are both productive and creative, and where established lines of communication always ensure that people are on the same page.

Unfortunately, not enough workplaces hold accountability as an important value. According to a workplace accountability Study by Partners in Leadership, 82 percent of survey respondents lamented that they didn't have the ability to hold their team members accountable. And they were certainly not happy about this; in fact, 91 percent ranked accountability at the top of their organization's needs.[1] Companies need to start paying attention to this; in the absence of systems of accountability or clearly delineated expectations, progress can be demonstrably hindered and collective team morale might suffer. Moreover, this creates environments in which some employees work extra hard but receive little to no recognition, while others might do the bare minimum and receive no reprimand in return. This can quickly create a frustrating and unsupportive work environment that discounts and negates the accomplishments of top performers while carrying the dead weight of negligent team members. The American Psychological Association noted that workers are more motivated and engaged when they sense that their company values them and their work.[2]

In addition, accountability leads to improved relationships among your team members, as they are assured that they can trust one another and that everyone will be doing their part to accomplish department or organizational goals. A culture of accountability also helps prevent a culture of assigning blame, which can all too quickly devolve into chaos rather than tenable solutions! If follow-through and problem-solving are emphasized, it's a lot less likely that team members will resort to the blame game.

One of the greatest reasons for leaders and companies to foster a culture of accountability is that it works! Productivity increases, especially when companies clearly articulate their goals, and roles and responsibilities are clearly meted out and communicated to employees. Another Partners in Leadership study discovered that nine out of ten companies didn't have clearly defined goals or hadn't communicated them effectively; because of this, 75 percent of their employees had no understanding of what their organization was trying to achieve or of what was expected of them.[3]

Of course, responsible organizations and the leaders they trust recognize that accountability reduces liability. For good reason, the stakes are higher when it comes to leaders and organizations maintaining impeccable reputations. Workplace policy and procedures, as well as trainings, that actively address topics like sexual harassment and racial discrimination, are essential—and leaders who are well versed in appropriate behavior at work can ensure that the office environment is a safe, respectful one that protects the organization and employees from potential liability risks. This also helps organizations keep a strict account of abuses of power and privilege and respond to them accordingly. Misconduct can be a major betrayal of trust within and beyond the organization, so having a system of ethical checks and balances not only ensures that everything is above board and people are held accountable, but it also ensures that team members will not be blamed for things they did not do.

x— Insight 18 → o

Build High-Performance Teams

One of the most important aspects of being a leader is managing the performance of your team and driving to results *through* others.

The higher you go in the organization, the more important this capability is. To be considered a high-performance leader, you must take time to ensure that you are clear on your organization's goals, and that you are familiar with the expectations that are inherent in your own role. You can do this in a number of ways.

- Prioritize the priorities! Performance expert Stephen Covey uses the metaphor of the big rocks theory. Essentially, if you have rocks, pebbles, and sand, and you take all that material and place it in a jar, the rocks will take up the most space. The pebbles and sand will fill the spaces between the rocks. The idea here is that you should put the rocks (the big and important tasks) into the jar first; then, you add the pebbles, and last, the sand.[4] As a leader, you have to focus on advancing the critical priorities to help your team achieve its goals.

- Assess your own skill set and that of the current team, which will help you determine whether or not you need to "manage up or manage out," which references the leadership principles of businessman, visionary, and entrepreneur Quint Studer. With the help of your HR department, you can figure this out. It means that, as a leader, your role is to consistently ensure that you're building up and supporting your team members to perform well. This should always start with role clarification, so that you are 100 percent certain that you and your team members are clear on expectations of performance. If they are not meeting expectations, you should work collaboratively with the team member and HR to develop a plan that will *support* their growth and future success. Understandably, nobody enjoys "managing out" poor performers; however, it's best to have these conversations proactively and as frequently as possible to ensure that such people are not dragging your team down, which could impact your ability to meet goals. In a *Business Insider* article about Steve Jobs, aptly titled "The Steve Jobs Guide to Manipulating People and Getting What You Want," something he often used to say stands out: "If something sucks, I tell people to their face. It's my job to be honest."[5] Although Jobs's overall approach left a lot to be desired (I certainly do not advocate the kind of manipulation the Apple founder was known for), there is something to be said for his statement. Whether or not you agree with Jobs's approach, developing people does not need to involve brutal honesty, but it does need to involve honesty. And it must be balanced with a sense of support and understanding. When you are developing your team, you have to incorporate a steady flow of positive reinforcement while also addressing when a team member is falling short of his or her potential.

- As you are evaluating your team, determine their strengths and opportunities for improvement and ensure that they have a solid plan that enables them to leverage their strengths. Provide them with support for their growth in the competencies that are critical for success in their roles. It is unfair for leaders to withhold critical feedback, no matter how difficult it is to share it, so that the person has the runway and the support from you to improve.

- "Hire slowly and fire quickly!" I don't know who coined that phrase, but the bottom line is that you should be extremely diligent and pragmatic with making hiring decisions and never wait to manage the performance of those on your team. If you have managed performance well and still have a person who is not meeting expectations, even after consistently providing support, feedback, and tools and resources, you need to cut the cord. It is up to you to be honest about performance gaps and their impact on not meeting organizational objectives.

- Use the following checklist to ensure that you are sustaining a high performance culture:
    - Be clear on your organization's goals and the metrics the organization is using.
    - Know your boss's priorities before you create yours, then write your goals in line with those of your boss.
    - Ensure that the team members who report to you also have goals aligned with yours and the timelines to achieve them.
    - Review your and your team's priorities regularly.
    - Write out new goals every ninety days, and ask your team to do the same.
    - Have frequent conversations with your boss to ensure alignment, especially as new priorities develop.
    - Have frequent conversations with your direct reports to ensure that they are making progress toward the goals.
        - If they are, be sure to praise, recognize, and reward them.
        - If they are not, what conversations can you have with them to get them back on track?

The best way to drive performance is to have clearly aligned goals. If you are not clear about what they are, it's likely that your organization lacks a process, or you and your boss are not having the right kinds of conversations around goal setting.

One organization I worked for utilized the 9-box model, a popular management tool in which leaders are divided into nine groups on the basis of their past performance and future potential.

The organization went through a specific process annually. Each leader had their own folder, which contained objective and measurable data on critical metrics, such as employee engagement results, patient experience results, and turnover rate; these data points were coupled with open and transparent conversation about each leader's strengths, capabilities, and opportunities for improvement. All the senior leaders were able to provide input, then each leader was placed into one of nine boxes on the whiteboard.

By the end of the process, we had a data-driven, transparent approach for ranking all the leaders. At that point, as senior leaders, we were expected to manage performance based on where the leader was placed. For example, if a leader was in the box indicating they were a high performer, our next steps were to attend to this by creating a plan for promotion within a defined timeframe. On the other hand, if a leader fell into the box of low performer/low potential, we were expected to work directly with HR to develop a plan for immediate performance improvement.

There are a number of similar tools, so it's important to determine which one fits with your organization. Although no tool is perfect, I highly recommend you utilize a process that is transparent, objective, and data-driven, and in which you have removed bias as much as possible.

One final word of advice is to ensure that the right people are in the right roles—this will make or break you as a leader. I recall a time when I observed that a high-ranking executive who had been a poor performer for years was able to move around within the organization. The person had a number of different one-up leaders who hadn't set him up for success. Additionally, this executive lacked clarity on the role he was to perform, and didn't know how to navigate all the stakeholders important to his role. All the while, he hadn't set up clear expectations for his own team, which meant their work was suffering as a result. The one thing this person did have was key relationships in the organization, making him almost untouchable, despite the fact that people complained how he'd out-lasted more effective leaders left and right. To this day, the leader remains in the same organization, albeit in yet a different role. If I had my guess, the individual likely hasn't improved much in the way of performance or leadership effectiveness and is on track to sail smoothly into retirement, which was his stated plan every time his one-up leader changed.

Make no mistake: people will make judgments about you and your ability to lead based on how you manage others—whether other leaders or individual contributors—including those who may have had reputations as "problem children" long before you arrived. In the words of Jim Collins in his book *Good to Great*, get "the right people on the bus, the wrong people off the bus, and the right people in the right seats."[6] This is perhaps one of the most crucial insights for ensuring your own success as a leader because no one person can drive results alone. Working through and with others is necessary, and your ability to have the best people on your team is paramount to your credibility and reputation as a high-per-forming leader.

x— Insight 19 → o

Drive to Results

As we've previously discussed, an important aspect of accountabil-ity is the ability to drive results and achieve tangible goals. The term *results-oriented* is an often overstated skill that is highlighted on thousands of résumés, but how many of those thousands of people understand what this actually entails? Talent goes beyond checking off items on a daily to-do list. It is not about pushing yourself to the brink of exhaustion to see how much you can get done. Being results-oriented is understanding that you achieve results with the help of your team, your colleagues, and—let's not forget—your entire village. For the context of this insight, it's important to focus on achieving results with collaboration and help from the teams you lead.

Achieving results starts with goal setting. After you've shared a larger vision with your team, the next step is allowing your team to develop *how* they will execute. Your role is to set the *clear* vision and allow your team the space to achieve it. I want to emphasize the importance of the word *clear* in this case, because employees can often feel that their company's objectives, or their own roles in fulfilling them, aren't transparent or self-explanatory.

Think of a time you walked into a conference room (virtual or otherwise) to gather for a meeting. As you took your seat, you noticed confusing remnants of the previous session on the dry-erase board: there shapes with arrows pointing in every direction and boxes filled with the text, "goal 1, goal 2, goal 3," and so on. You may have questioned the purpose of that meeting. You may have even felt sorry for those who had to endure the previous session—or you may have encountered similar convoluted diagrams in your own meetings! Countless journals and articles present ways to develop objectives to achieve desired results. The number of practices does not ultimately matter. What does matter, however, is that the goals are easy to follow and measure. Clear objectives and key results are a "shared language for execution."[7]

In *Measure What Matters*, author John Doerr calls these shared language OKRs, objectives and key results.[8] Doerr presents an easy method to develop quarterly objectives as a team with key action steps to achieve each objective. For the leader and the team, this method makes it easy to identify who is accountable for specific action steps. When the time arrives for the quarterly results to be measured, the method can quickly help figure out who the poor performers are, and accordingly, ensure that there is accountability.

Let's break down this OKR method. Let's say you are creating a list of objectives for your team. You would write an objective at the top of your list; below it, you'd add three to five specific supporting key results. Here's an example: "I will [fill in the blank with your objective], and my success will be measured by [fill in the blank with your desired key results]." An objective is simply what you are looking to achieve, and it should be concrete. Ideally, it should also inspire your team members enough to drive to your key results, which should be specific, measurable, and realistic. The great thing about defining key results is you're not leaving any ambiguity or room for doubt (even though you've ideally mastered the ability to navigate ambiguity, if you hearken back to Insight 15!). If you achieve your key results, you will absolutely know that you did.

It's important to note again that creating a culture of account-ability is best done when all your efforts are collaborative. You aim to develop your objectives collectively, which can generate mean-ingful discussion that initiates curious questions and flags any exist-ing concerns. If you are establishing your objectives effectively, all team members should leave each meeting feeling clear, motivated, and more confident about their ability to drive to results than they did when they walked into the room.

"All **business is personal**. . . .

Make your **friends before**

you need them."

—Robert L. Johnson, entrepreneur

CHAPTER 9

Treating Relationships as Golden

A playbook for excelling as a leader in corporate America would be incomplete without a chapter on the importance of relationships. Carla Harris, the talented Wall Street executive, coined the term *relationship currency*, which is the most valuable currency that you can have in any environment.[1] I've already alluded to this throughout the book, but career relationships influence a leader's efficacy; hence, any good leader will acknowledge that, throughout their tenure, their achievements were only possible because of the help they received from many others. This assistance encompasses working with others by way of special projects, being introduced to others for the sake of building networks, being mentored and supported by people who act as cheerleaders for your vision—the list goes on. All these relationships have likely afforded you the opportunity to hear specific feedback about your strengths and opportunities to grow, solidify your vision, and contribute meaningfully on plum assignments or committee work.

As a leader, you must always remember that influence is king and that wielding influence requires learning how to manage up, down, and across an organization. The ability to influence is an important capability, regardless of the level you inhabit within your company. However, the higher you go in leadership, the more important your ability to influence others becomes.

The critical managerial relationship around influencing others can be broken into three buckets: your boss (managing up), your peers (managing across), and your direct reports (managing down).

Managing up is all about the influence you have with your boss—there is no greater influence, positive or negative, than the one you have with your one-up leader. If you do not build and intentionally cultivate a productive relationship with your boss, you're toast! I see it over and over, and have experienced it myself. The absence of a productive working relationship with your one-up leader can be absolutely detrimental not only to your ability to influence within your organization, but also to your career trajectory within the organization—period. Therefore, building an enriching relationship with your boss has to be a priority. This step is often overlooked in career-building, because it may appear to some that establishing rapport with your leader can be more of a gesture of flattery than a meaningful step toward success. However, an effective relationship with your boss can develop into a partnership wherein they become your ally, especially in the case of promotions. The lack of a productive working relationship with the person you report to can be harmful to your ability to influence the organization and stunt your career trajectory within the company.

A Black male HR executive shared the following about the importance of this relationship. "Spend time with your one-up leader and understand how the person works, how he communicates, and how he wants to be communicated with. For example, some want a quick note each day, others might want you to reach out every week, or even every other week. Know that communication with your leader is key and then know that the level of prioritization of what he is working on can shift easily. You need to be in lockstep with those shifting priorities so that you and your team are helping your leader achieve and be more effective. I think about it this way: If a leader has a team full of people focused on the organizational objectives, driving execution around those objectives, and then his priorities, it is easier for everyone to be aligned and move in the same direction."

Managing across is the ability to work productively with and even influence your peers. Working with your peers across the organization is a skill that is as important as working effectively with your own one-up leader. This is where office politics can sometimes come into play (more about that in the next chapter). Learning who the informal power players are—with and without titles—is crucial, especially early on. It is best for you to determine who all your peers are, as well as the ones you will need to have as allies. Your peers can help or hinder you, especially when it comes to your relationship with your boss and other key stakeholders. It's important to focus on building positive working relationships with your peers across the organization, in different departments and functional areas. Having a number of people whose brains you can pick and with whom you can collaborate on projects makes it easier for you to get your own projects across the finish line. Putting the effort into developing and nurturing these trusted relationships with peers will do wonders for your role, so invest the time to do this, as these are alliances you will undoubtedly need.

Finally, *managing down* is all about the influence you have on your direct reports. Regardless of whether or not you consider yourself a people person, cementing your position with your team takes time and skill. The first step is building trust, setting clear expectations, and holding your team accountable both collectively and individually. Mutual respect, support, transparency, and leading with heart and compassion are all key attributes of strong connections with your team. As much as people want a solid leader who has vision and the ability to secure resources, your team is counting on you to be there as an emotionally intelligent human first—someone who values humanity over numbers or sales goals.

Once trust is established, your team will gladly abide by expectations, adopt your vision, and look forward to being held accountable for their contribution to the team's success. There are some specific tactics I would recommend to help you develop relationships with your direct reports.

If you are new to your role, start out by visiting, with no agenda, with each person on your team. Share about your background, family, what drives you, and your vision and goals. Get to know the other person as much as they are comfortable sharing. Building the relationship based on what makes the other person happy will yield you some deposits in the emotional bank account. Then, in successive meetings, ask them about their family and likes, then continue the relationship from there. Even if you have been in your role for some time, start now by engaging on a personal level to find some common ground and connection. The key here is connection—everyone wants community and engagement—and the time you spend on the front end, showing that you are interested in the relationships with your direct reports, will yield dividends.

For women and people of color especially, the concept of relationship capital is critical, and the ability to build significant influence cannot be underestimated. Often, these demographics tend to have fewer doors open to them compared with white colleagues. History and reality have shown repeatedly that many interlocked oppressive systems have shut out even the most educated, highly qualified people of color from significant opportunities. Many organizations are starting to redress decades of lack of opportunity with meaningful and substantive diversity, equity, and inclusion initiatives; some include specific incentives for more leaders of color to be hired in decision-making roles. Consider this: although the United States is comparatively more diverse than other nations, with Blacks making up 12 percent of the population, grim statistics exist for key roles in organizations. According to the Center for Talent Innovation's Race to Lead study, Black people inhabit 3.2 percent of senior leadership roles at large companies and 0.8 percent of all Fortune 500 CEO positions; moreover, 65 percent of Blacks said they feel they have to work harder for advancement opportunities compared with only 16 percent of white employees.[2]

Let's expand our discussion of influence capability by addressing the notion of the *sphere of influence*. What does this mean? It is the manner in which you work through others to execute plans that will ultimately drive results. We can reword that by saying that, as a leader, you achieve goals through the people on your team. However, your sphere of influence extends beyond your team and becomes relationship currency.[3]

In a recent article, Carla Harris notes that relationship currency is "generated by the investments that you make in the people in your environment." She goes on to say that because we all work in interdependent environments, we must ensure that we are garnering influence with others in the organization, not just our boss. She suggests four key steps to building relationship currency, particularly in the post-COVID world:[4]

- **Initiate outreach.** If you want to build a relationship with someone, reach out to them for a video chat or phone call for a minimum of fifteen minutes (since it can be difficult to sustain a longer conversation if you don't know them well or might not have enough material for a longer conversation).
- **Establish a clear agenda.** Give the person you're talking to a sense of what you'd like to discuss so they can be prepared and also feel that the time was efficiently spent.
- **Come prepared.** Come with specific questions you have for the person you'll be talking with; for example, you might want to ask them about essential skills and training

that you should consider as you move forward in your career.

- **Be grateful.** Always be sure to follow up with a gracious thank you to this person for their time!

Remember, the ability to influence others is an invaluable skill to possess, regardless of your career level. In the words of John C. Maxwell, "Leadership is influence. Nothing more. Nothing Less."[5]

x– Insight 20 → o

Show Appreciation

One of the most important ways you can nurture your relationships in the workplace is to express appreciation and gratitude for those with whom you work. Sounds like a no-brainer, right? It is certainly one of the most straightforward actions a leader can take on any given day. But how often is it actually done?

Expressing gratitude coincides with being curious about the members of your team. In order for the expression to be authentic, you must know *what* you are thanking your team members for. Your words must be specific to the action, because this displays more emotion and sends the message to your team members that you gave their effort adequate attention. It also lets your team members know that you are not receiving information secondhand; you care about recognizing your team's efforts. For example, instead of merely saying, "Thanks for doing that!" begin the gratitude statement with, "I noticed that you [fill in the blank with their specific action]," or "I like how you approached [note the issue that was addressed or resolved by the team member]."

What can you as a leader recognize your team members for? Aside from recognizing them for achieving goals, you can acknowledge people for becoming subject-matter experts. Of course, it's easy to appreciate a high performer, but you can also show gratitude toward the team member who has made marked improvements in their work. Be creative in your methods and mindful to choose a recognition technique that coincides with what you know about the people on your team.

The following are a few examples of how you can show appreciation to your team.

- Consider handwritten thank-you notes with specific, personal messages.
- Ask your leaders and other staff if there's anyone they would like to recognize, and use this as an opportunity to say thank you to the staff member via email, handwritten note, or other method.
- Offer personalized gifts and rewards, which demonstrate that you've paid attention and know something about the team member's passions and interests.
- Bring in small and simple treats, like doughnuts, a fruit platter, or other fun surprises.
- Support your team members' personal and professional development by offering them opportunities to spread their wings, perhaps with training seminars in subjects that interest them or by allowing them to attend conferences to fulfill the continuing education needs they have.

Overall, when expressing appreciation, be both sincere and consistent. Don't wait for special occasions to show your appreciation. Say thank you often and take the time to recognize and reward your team for a job well done.

x— *Insight 21* → o

Be a Highly Engaged and Good Team Player

During team meetings, you might often hear leaders toss around the word *we*. While verbalizing the power of "we" is significant, the action behind the words is what makes all the difference. There is no "we" if a leader is not present on the front lines of business operations.

This means that you are truly visible, not just a figurehead within the organization whose door is literally and metaphorically closed so that your team members can't adequately access you. You also use existing organizational channels to achieve a meaningful presence for your team members, which includes infusing your voice in all communications (from department emails to team meetings) and setting up regular check-ins with individual team members so that you demonstrate you are fully engaged in everything that is happening across your organization.

Receiving feedback from your team is crucial, but observing for yourself allows you to see, in real time, the processes that are working exceptionally well and what needs to be optimized. Planned recognitions are meaningful, as we noted in the last insight, and they add value and increase morale. A visible leader can congratulate people in the moment of their accomplishments, making those announcements even more authentic.

As a leader, being engaged and reminding everyone that you're all on the same team extends from evaluating performance (not to mention, creating plans that enable improved performance) to determining where more creativity can be applied in your organizational or departmental processes. Increasing your visibility will provide knowledge of what positions and responsibilities will challenge everyone around you more.

Being visible keeps your high performers prepared and eager to grow, because your genuine presence and attention demonstrate that you care about the work of your team members. However, increasing your presence isn't about micromanaging. It's about expressing curiosity regarding your team members' work and providing opportunities for them to share their feedback and suggestions. It's also about offering the kind of guidance and insight that enables your team members to reach their potential and make them feel fully engaged with your company's goals. When you are engaging appropriately and with intention, you ensure that your team members feel needed, valued, appreciated, and similarly engaged. This motivates them to bring more of their ideas and expertise to the table, because your visibility is going to inspire them to move toward greater success. This is a recipe for improved performance across the board!

Dreams do come true, but not without the **help of others**, a **good education**, a **strong work ethic**, and the courage to lean in.

—Ursula Burns, former CEO of Xerox and first Black woman CEO of a Fortune 500 company

CHAPTER 10

Understanding Advocates, Mentors, and Sponsors as Levers for Career Success

No leader succeeds in a vacuum; the efforts of countless people are connected to their success. "It takes a village to raise a child" is a popular African proverb and has been adopted by many in the African American community as a popular reference. This proverb can easily be applied to career advancement. How? As a leader, you have a team of employees with whom you interact daily within the workplace. Then, you have your village.

Wall Street veteran Carla Harris talked about this in a popular TED Talk she gave in 2019. She shared that during business school, she was told that the way to build a successful career was by putting your head down and working hard. After sitting through a meeting in which employees, without their knowledge, were being ranked on their promotability, Harris realized that putting her head down was not going to get her anywhere. Her primary objective became building a network of people who would advocate for her, especially during a meeting like the one she had sat through![1]

There are three different kinds of people who might serve as important pillars in your team of champions.

Take a moment to reflect on some of the individuals you've met at different stages in your career growth. At the beginning of your career, you likely met someone you were able to share your challenges with and gleaned advice on improving certain tasks and attaining skill sets specific to your industry and position. This person acted not only as your sounding board, but also offered helpful advice on ways to uncover your strengths and new ways to approach and solve challenges. While you appreciated the value and the connection you made with these individuals and the support they gave you during your career progression, your relationship with them was not static. The level of skill these people carried progressed as you progressed. This served you well, for as you moved forward in your career, you needed progressive advice that would also take you to each new level you achieved. These individuals serve as *mentors*. They are typically people who have achieved the level of success that you seek. Your mentor might be someone in your workplace or not; in addition, they might be in the same industry or perhaps a different sector. You can approach this individual for advice on how to navigate the workplace. You can learn from them which resources to use to expand your skill set. You can also bare your heart to them by expressing any fears or insecurities on your advancement journey, and you can receive their words of wisdom.

One of my interviewees, a Black male executive, shared the power of a professional mentoring relationship he had with another Black male in the company, whose fearlessness in sharing difficult feedback made a positive impact. "I had an approximately one-hour commute each way to work, and my first day I arrived at work three minutes late. The next day, I left home an hour and forty-five minutes early; however, there was an accident on the way, and I was again a few minutes late. This leader called me into his office, and needless to say, we had a challenging conversation around my commitment. After that, I showed up at 6:30 a.m. for six straight months. Then this same individual came by my desk and said, 'I think you got it—you can shoot to arrive at 7:00 a.m.' We had a great relationship, and to me, that was mentorship at its finest, filled with a great lesson early in my career that has served me well since."

Because he was reporting to another Black male, my interviewee also felt an extra responsibility to not "mess up." After probing deeper his comment, which had resonated with me, he went on to explain that "a number of Black professionals carry the weight of the world on our shoulders." In some ways, while that weight can be a cross to bear, interactions between BIPOC mentors and their BIPOC mentees can be a powerful way of mirroring our excellence to each other and harnessing a deeper sense of accountability.

Now that you've thought about someone who supported you in the early stages of your career, think for a moment about a person who possesses the talents, insight, and emotional intelligence to reach exceptional heights in their own career. This individual has the influence to open doors for others because of where they sit—at the senior level within a company. Perhaps this person may have even created an opportunity for you that you may not have been able to garner on your own. People such as these serve as *sponsors*. The terms *mentor* and *sponsor* are often used interchangeably, but their primary purposes are different. A sponsor can fill the role of a mentor with an added layer of promoting you and giving you critical "cover" you need to help you be successful. While mentors offer you much-needed and well-timed guidance, sponsors intentionally push for your development and advancement by advocating for you in meetings that you do not even know exist! Usually, a sponsor is at least two levels above where you are within the organization; this is especially important as you think about the dynamics of how high-visibility opportunities for projects, committee assignments, promotions and new roles, and even compensation are managed within the corporate environment. Sponsors have the authority, influence, respect, and power to help you advance. Start to think about these distinctions as you look around your own organization for those who could serve as potential sponsors.

For women, and especially women of color, sponsorship is a critical component of career advancement strategy. One of the lines etched in my memory is the notion that women tend to be "over-mentored and under-sponsored" meaning that they may have a bevy of mentors but not enough sponsors to open the doors of advancement opportunity to move up.

Let's revisit Carla Harris. As she spoke about her experience of sitting in the private meeting held to rank employees, she focused on the fact that, as names were called, people in the discussion either approved or disapproved of these employees. The approval or disapproval was independent of job performance and instead based on the perception of personalities. Harris left the meeting, realizing she needed more than a mentor; she needed a sponsor. A sponsor is the "person carrying your interest, carrying your paper into the room . . . spending their valuable political and social capital, and pounding the pavement on your behalf." Essentially, a sponsor is a person who gets invited into those private meetings like the one Harris described.[2]

Finally, I want to talk about *career advocates*. These are people who are your fans and who continue to rave about you, perhaps offering word-of-mouth referrals to others and providing you with opportunities you may not have previously considered. Your village outside of the workplace might consist of career advocates, as they are your peers and colleagues or even friends whom you can count on to encourage you with words, support your vision, and celebrate your wins. Career advocates might also be mentors or sponsors, but they are not necessarily either of these.

Overall, having a mentor and sponsor at any stage of your career is highly advantageous. One person can serve in both roles. These roles matter greatly and should not be overlooked as a part of your career plan. People have to be aware of you—hearing your name should spark interest because they know you and your work. The ability to move higher in any career is a function of someone's judgment on your readiness, your chances of being successful, and your influence—judgment is influenced by relationships.

It is common knowledge that when discussions occur around promotions, the meetings are held behind closed and locked doors, with the keys hidden! During these meetings, several names are mentioned as candidates for said promotion. To even have your name voiced in the meeting, someone has to know you. Often, people spend so much time building their skills and obtaining degrees, certificates, and extra training, they forget to network altogether. While all those aspects are certainly of massive importance, networking cannot be the last item on your priority list. If you are reading this book at the start of your career, place networking in the number-one spot on your "how to get ahead in my career" list!

Building relationships through sponsorship and mentorship is of utmost importance for leaders of color because, frankly, we are still overlooked in organizations. Miia Suokonautio, the executive director of YWCA Halifax, states, "Mentorship is an act of social justice; you are re-investing into your mentee the resources and privileges invested in you. Consider how you can bring about justice by who you mentor."[3]

Although Miia's statement is often directed toward leaders and mentorship, we can apply it to sponsorship as well. It's a lesson for companies committed to establishing a culture in which leaders of color are the norm, to view sponsorship and mentorship opportunities as an avenue to eradicate racial inequalities within corporate settings.

Building your village—specifically, your mentors and sponsors—begins with your willingness to put yourself in settings you might usually bypass. The purpose is to be seen, even if it means networking outside the office. In her book *The Memo*, Minda Harts gives a great example of the "going to happy hour after work" scenario. In the past, you may have turned down this type of invitation. Harts tells the story of an employee forcing herself—she didn't really want to—to join her colleagues and a few people on the leadership team for happy hour. This employee accepts the invitation a few additional times and, soon after, receives a promotion. There are a few gripes in the company about this employee's promotion because there are others who are more qualified for the position. While that might be true, the leadership team had developed a connection with the chosen employee. Simply put, she was in the right place at the right time, which enabled leaders to build trust in her.[4] That isn't all it takes, of course, but it can be a key that opens that closed door!

x— Insight 22 → o

Get Noticed by Potential Sponsors

A career without sponsors isn't going to get you very far, so here are four powerful ways to get yourself noticed by potential sponsors within your organization and industry.

- Build relationships and have a consistent focus on driving results and performing well in the job you have *today*. It is particularly important to develop relationships with those who are one to two levels higher than you in your organization; this might include your direct supervisor as well as their direct supervisor. In fact, continue to cultivate the relationship with your boss and ensure that they are advocating for you. I specifically talk about one to two levels above you because this is where the critical conversations about promotions and compensation take place.

- Don't be shy! Speak up and share your career goals with others. But also, be very strategic about how, where, and with whom you share your goals. Sponsors can't show up for you if they don't know what you're seeking.
- Get involved in employee groups that focus on specific ethnicities and demographics, not just your own. This can create a more open discussion on ways the organization can be more culturally competent—not to mention, you'll receive greater visibility as an effective collaborator.
- If you are new to an organization or your role, identifying the influencers within your particular sector is a step you do not want to overlook. It is also crucial to know that, sometimes, those who have power and influence in a company don't always hold titles or the top positions. This is where having a broad network is particularly helpful.

Building your village, specifically with respect to mentors and sponsors, can assist you in navigating workplace dynamics, otherwise known as workplace politics, which we'll discuss in greater depth in the next chapter. On my leadership journey, I have come to grasp that leadership and aspirations toward leadership require that we accept political savviness as an important attribute to build in the workplace. This can help us become more adept in identifying and connecting with those who will champion us when necessary. Whether you work for a large corporation or in a small office, ignoring this part of your career advancement could result not only in your forfeiting opportunities, but also in dismissing important relationships with potential mentors and sponsors.

A Black male executive in the finance industry shared with me that he wished he'd been more aware of the importance of sponsorship, particularly as a man of color in the corporate world. "I haven't taken some chances or risks because of playing it safe," he confessed. "We know that we need to take risks sometimes in order to get to that next big role or more or different types of responsibility. Somehow, deep within, I believe from what I have observed that I wouldn't have the same level of grace if I took a risk and failed at something, versus one of my white male colleagues. My point is that there was a bit of a limitation on my career by not taking things that I wasn't 100 percent comfortable with because I didn't feel like I had the support or the backing that would sustain me in case things didn't go well in the role." This is why, as a leader of color, it's especially powerful to understand how helpful it can be to have cheerleaders who recognize your value and are willing to go to bat for you, and usually this comes with sponsorship. Don't just seek out mentors, but focus on your career in a way that you are also being sought out by sponsors who will help you navigate and also call your name out for opportunities to advance.

x— Insight 23 → o

Learn When and When Not to Self-Promote

In the discussion of creating our village, the notion of self-promotion is paramount for women and BIPOC, who must be relentlessly intentional when it comes to gaining the proverbial seat at the table.

The happy-hour scenario mentioned earlier is only one way to make yourself known. Even though personalities come into play regarding promotions, job performance remains at the top of the list when it comes to getting noticed. As you build your village, consider how you complete projects and assignments. Do you inform whom you report to that you have completed the task? Or do you take the extra step to schedule some time not only to present your project but also to request feedback? Keep in mind that how and the frequency with which you inform depends on your leader and the culture of your organization.

Think about how you approach meetings. Do you prepare ahead of time with thoughtful questions? When the space is open to offer feedback, do you take advantage of that time to provide solutions that would benefit your team? These behaviors get noticed and keep your name at the top of all minds.

You need to be comfortable sharing your achievements and results, regardless of your career level. If you are currently a leader, maintain the practice of excitedly describing your career trajectory. If you are not a leader yet, or if you have just entered the corporate landscape, get into the habit of sharing your current successes. Even if it feels forced, as you advance, this will become second nature. You will have developed ways to share your success, not in an obnoxious or egocentric manner, but in a way that is advantageous to your career. Sharing your expertise influences others at all career levels to appreciate your value and work, even if you work differently from most. If you bypass this essential skill, you risk being overlooked.

The cold truth about any organization is that great work can easily go unnoticed. This is where self-promotion comes in—a double-edged sword that involves striking a balance between modesty and hubris.

Over the course of my career, I have talked with many leaders of color about self-promotion. We are taught at a very early age to not appear arrogant in the workplace. I find humility an admirable quality that I look for in other leaders, and I try my best to be humble. However, we must learn to be humble without hiding behind our accomplishments or otherwise downplaying our journey.

Good self-promotion is all about confidently highlighting your value and impact on the organization without being off-putting or self-congratulatory. Getting self-promotion wrong can be off-putting to those around you, therefore you have to know when and when not to go for it. One of the common challenges I see is when leaders don't want to appear overconfident, cocky, or arrogant, so they sometimes miss the opportunity to showcase and highlight their accomplishments.

Following are specific tips on how to do self-promotion the right way.

- **Keep a record of your work.** I have always advocated for employees, and especially leaders, to keep a job diary that contains the good, the bad, and the ugly about their projects, experiences, and lessons learned. Not only is it helpful and sometimes even therapeutic to be able to download your experiences into written form, but you can also learn from one experience or one role to the next about what happened, how you responded and reacted, and the outcomes. These experiences can be powerful lessons for you to revisit.

- **Be focused.** Test the waters of self-promotion only if you are focused and intentional about your workplace end goal. Instead of trying to showcase every single achievement, pick specific successes that align with your end goal. For example, if you want greater responsibilities in the area of customer satisfaction, focus on self-promoting your impact in this area, and avoid being a master of all other competencies. You can only be effective at so much!

- **Bring others along.** Self-promote when you are capable of making others look good as well. Nobody likes the persistent horn tooter. Recognize the contributions of everyone who helped you achieve a goal. Additionally, the easiest way to self-promote is to offer your services to your peers and leaders. By becoming an asset to everyone, you can demonstrate your talents without coming off as a braggart.

- **Ask for feedback.** Self-promotion works effectively when there is a strong feedback loop in your workplace. This way, your boss, supervisors, and clients can see your wins clearly and talk about them. By asking for feedback, you create room for your successes to be discussed in detail. However, be prepared to receive criticisms as well as praises.

- **Volunteer for visible *and promotable* tasks.** Self-promotion is all about visibility, appreciation, and acknowledgment for making a difference and adding value for your organization. Your time to shine opens up when you put yourself in a position to solve complex issues and problems within the organization in a collaborative manner.

- **Come with results.** Never blow your own trumpet if you cannot demonstrate clear results. Recognize your strengths and weaknesses and use them to your advantage. However, you should never limit yourself. Be prepared to shift beyond your comfort zone.

- **Share your wins with your leader.** Keep track of your accomplishments and, when you are meeting with your leader, take a moment to share how you are driving results for the organization. Also, share what you are working on outside of work. For example, if you are in a leadership role in a professional organization or on the board of a local nonprofit, share some of this work with your leader and colleagues. It shows that you have depth and are engaged and involved; it also shows that other organizations recognize the strength of your leadership brand.

- **Leverage social media.** If you've mastered the art of building a solid brand, you know that putting yourself out there with social media requires persistence, tenacity, and creativity. Flex your self-promotion muscle by using social media platforms to share your professional experience and successes. Platforms such as LinkedIn and even Instagram can be used skillfully to help you leverage your accomplishments at your workplace or in the community and build your personal brand.

- **Perfect the art of the humble brag.** Nick Nelson, founder of The BRANDPRENUER Agency®, shared with me that a person can be humble and still brag. "One of my spirit animals is Muhammad Ali. People loved and hated him because he came into the mindset of talking to people about 'how great I am.' People understood that there was a showmanship about Ali, but they also understood that there was a humility around him as well, because he cared about people; rather than doing this for him, he was doing this for his people. He understood the gravity of being the heavyweight champion of the world, what that meant in terms of the prize and an image of Black people (more specifically here in the US), and how that image carried itself abroad. He was a great example of the humble brag." To tie it back to corporate, Nelson notes that it's important to never attempt to outshine your organization. "One of the things that I tell all my clients who work in corporate environments is that part of your personal branding is to absolutely make certain that your immediate manager is in lockstep with you, so that there are no surprises." Be humble, but also shine and share what you are doing![5]

Overall, self-promotion is an art form that can take some time to master. Depending on how you utilize it, you might be perceived as either a major asset or a self-centered phony. There is a thin line between failure and success, but you have to be brave enough to go for it—and course-correct when needed!

$x-$ *Insight 24* $\rightarrow$ o

Grow Other Leaders

Since you chose to be a leader, I'm going to assume that you are dedicated to investing time in preparing others for career and leadership success. However, you can only be effective in coaching and developing others when you have invested in yourself, and having done so makes it easy to recognize the potential in others. When we function in any leadership role, we need to think of ways to pass the torch to those around us who are capable.

As you develop your team, you are essentially inspiring members to step out of their comfort zone and utilize their talents at total capacity. Preparing others elevates their levels of autonomy. Developing your team also establishes a sense of freedom. From here, delegating becomes a simple process because your team will gather independently to manage portions of a project to completion. It also establishes more trust in you as a leader, because your team is confident in your commitment to helping them advance.

Overall, your work in developing the people on your team affects outcomes. Because of coaching, team members are willing to take on projects that may not have been in their initial purview. But with additional training, they now have the skills needed to take the lead on a particular project.

Whether you are engaging in development with the team or

presenting advancement opportunities to individuals, you must aim to approach everyone with the mindset that they want to advance in their role and personal development.

Let's dive into some solutions you can use and implement to create a culture where Black leaders advance.

- **Develop shadowing programs.** Such programs are not just for the sake of having an employee watch what another employee does and then return to their everyday work activities. Companies should create formal programs with a tangible outcome. After the shadowing period is complete, there needs to be a specific and undeniable advancement opportunity present.[6]

- **Develop sponsorship programs.** Identify prospective leaders in the organization and create a space for introductions to set sponsorship relationships in motion. This will set the tone for support and eliminate awkwardness, especially if the professionals have never met each other. If additional projects are assigned during the sponsorship programs, work with leaders to adjust their workloads. Companies should ensure that managers support their team members' initiative to advance. The point of such programs is to provide expansion not undue stress.

- **Provide executive coaching.** People with promotion potential should be matched with leadership or executive coaches who can help them delineate a plan for advancement and offer meaningful guidance in helping to amplify their capabilities, over and above what can be offered internally with the leader's one-up supervisor. In addition to you providing coaching to your team members, ensuring that they have a good coach can be a wonderful way to provide them with support for their professional development goals.

- **Offer regular training.** Because we know that BIPOC disproportionately bear the brunt of implicit bias, microaggressions, and systemic oppression, it's crucial to create opportunities for advancement for individuals in this group. Providing professional development training opportunities for all leaders, but especially for BIPOC leaders, is critical to helping those who are often overlooked for advancement. As a leader, you can advocate for training that helps other leaders understand their own biases and how these might be adversely impacting BIPOC.

Companies should ensure that leaders are equipped with the tools and resources to be effective, as well as invest in programs and initiatives to grow the competence and capability of their leaders. Especially in the current environment, organizations that offer robust professional and leadership development opportunities can leverage these tools to engage and retain mission-critical talent.

Sometimes **people try to destroy you**, precisely because they recognize your power—not because they don't see it, but **because they see it and don't want it to exist**.

—bell hooks, author

Navigating Corporate Politics

*N*ow we come to the topic of corporate politics, which any and every leader must learn to master if they wish to stay afloat within their organization. If you work in a company with more than two or three people, at some point, politics will be at play. The larger the organization, the more chances you will have to encounter politics. Add to that the often unspoken struggle that many BIPOC leaders experience, and the chess game becomes even more complex, especially the higher you go in the organization. Whether you like it or not, your career depends on your ability to maneuver successfully around workplace dynamics and politics.

You can find countless descriptions of the meaning of *organizational dynamics*. I define them as the continuous observations of how people interact with each other within a company. They can also be defined as the study of navigating around and coexisting with humans who have emotions in the workplace—in other words, everyone! One such example of organizational dynamics can be found in meetings. Observation encompasses where people sit, who is speaking, who is asking questions, and who is assertive and confident enough to offer suggestions about the topic at hand; all these offer meaningful insight into the dynamics of that particular company. We can even expand this into watching how other staff members respond to the people who are talking. Is there a person who receives more attention than others? Noting everyone's facial expressions and body language, including the leadership team, can also reveal information about where and how people are placed within the hierarchy of an organization, whether that hierarchy is overt or not.

Organizational dynamics are important because they give us direct knowledge about corporate politics and the unwritten rules that are at the core of this book. As I've mentioned in previous chapters, understanding the playbook about career and leadership success may seem like a game that we'd rather not partake in, but the more we are privy to the unwritten and unspoken rules, the better we will be able to navigate corporate spaces.

So, what are these unwritten rules? They are the workplace norms and behaviors that are not necessarily formalized in any organizational chart but are implicitly understood as the blueprint successful people in the company follow. Rather than being impediments, these organizational dynamics, when navigated with care, can facilitate our career advancement. They can also help us expand our confidence when interacting with others' emotions. The key is to take incremental steps. When we have established a pattern of observing workplace politics and understanding the playbook, we can respond to any situation with emotional intelligence and humanity—and still propel our careers.

Let's turn our attention to exploring some ways to become and remain keen in handling corporate politics. First, consider taking inventory or making observations of everything that happens in your workplace. Observing will help you understand the authentic culture of the organization, not the one that was presented to you during your job interview. Think about Insight 10 (communicate impactfully and listen actively). When you listen to the language people use, remember that body language is a significant aspect of communication and highlights a person's true feelings and thoughts. Allow me to emphasize here the importance of investing in communication improvement. Sensitivity to and understanding body language can be learned. As you seek resources to improve your communication, keep in mind that a thorough communication course will include training on how to interpret body language.

Another tip for navigating corporate politics is to pay close attention to promotion changes and leadership appointments. This will help you pinpoint whom you need to know and add to your network. People who understand workplace politics make it their business to know the key influencers, and even better, build relationships with them.

Remaining productive in the midst of workplace politics also involves the ability to recognize what gets rewarded and given positive acknowledgment, and what gets neglected altogether. This is especially important when it comes to promotions. You have to be clear and confident about the value you can add to the organization, department, or project you would like to be a part of.

As you build your network, continue to take stock of your assets. Even when you have a network of people willing and able to speak on your behalf, others within your organization need to hear you speak up for your skills as well. Although you may yet have the entire gamut of skills you need, you still need to express the competencies you *do* possess as well as your willingness to learn more. The heavy hitters in your organization smile upon people who are not afraid to share their accomplishments and what they can offer to the team. If you cannot voice what you bring to the boardroom or conference room, you will not build confidence in the others with whom you are attempting to increase your visibility.

We may feel a sense of relief when we have reached a level in our career that was always our aim. While we should take a moment to celebrate our wins, we must remain politically savvy in the workplace. Regardless of our leadership level, we must continue to be vigilant to our surroundings, paying attention to daily changes. We cannot fall into the trap of complacency or believe our position exempts us from workplace politics.

As a leader, becoming and remaining politically savvy can seem like an extra chore or yet another task on your to-do list. But remember, this is a process that will quickly feel less like work and more like a natural aspect of your approach to leading and working with others. Being successful in navigating workplace dynamics while still building a career you enjoy involves allowing yourself to observe small things from day to day. You do not have to conquer the entire organization at once—allow yourself incremental astuteness in political savviness.

x— Insight 25 → o

Manage Toxic Bosses Skillfully

When navigating corporate politics, it's instrumental to consider the role toxic leaders play. The movie *Horrible Bosses* shows the exaggerated plight of employees who struggle to survive workdays amid the treachery of their manipulative leader. Then, there's the cult film *Office Space*, which shows the trickle-down effect of micromanagement and the promotion and firing chaos that leads to the outrageous actions of employees who "get back" at the entire company. Or, take the 1980s comedy *9 to 5*, in which three secretaries are denied promotions and decide to kidnap their boss and take over his company. We may laugh and shake our heads at the hijinks, but are the behaviors of the so-called leaders in these movies all that different from what we hear in real life, what so many have witnessed and experienced, and what are fueling at least some part of the phenomenon known as the "great resignation" that started in 2021? According to a CBS News segment, "well over twenty million people quit their jobs in the second half of 2021."[1] The great resignation has had and will continue to impact every sector of the workforce.

According to a *Fast Company* article about the great resignation, a group of researchers asked employees about the likelihood of their quitting their jobs; the majority reported that feeling undervalued in their workplace was a top reason (2 percent of respondents cited this as a top reason for quitting). However, a significant number (18 percent) also noted that having a bad supervisor increased the likelihood of quitting a job.[2]

Of course, having a bad supervisor is one thing, but what takes a leader from "bad" to "toxic"? It's likely that, although they might be a high achiever, which has enabled them to get ahead, they lack integrity, emotional intelligence, or, as I like to say, lack just plain heart and compassion for people. Imagine working for a leader who, for their own benefit, gaslighted their direct reports or others within the organization; or a leader who had such a mercurial personality that you never knew whether you were getting the nice leader, the angry leader, the fed-up leader, or the moody leader. Imagine what it's like to work for a person who peppers conversations and meetings with sarcasm and condescending comments, or repeatedly berates and belittles you during meetings, or worse yet, excludes you from meetings altogether and tries to damage your credibility by manipulating conversations with your peers and other influencers within the company.

Believe it doesn't happen? Think again. Unfortunately, I have observed these behaviors and even experienced some of them myself. How do these leaders remain in their roles, wreaking havoc on the psyches of those with whom they work?

A Black male HR executive I spoke with noted, "What I found in my career is that almost every organization knows who the bad leaders are, and unfortunately, they tolerate them for a variety of reasons. Don't put yourself in a situation where you are suffering from an ineffective or toxic leader, and you aren't doing anything about it. I've always advocated for individuals to bring those issues up—you know, take a risk. If you are at a Fortune 500 company and things are not working out, there are 499 other ones. Life is too short to stay and be completely miserable working with a toxic boss."

We may think of a toxic leader as loud, obnoxious, or harboring other unfavorable behaviors. But underlying toxicity might not be that blatant; many aspects of a leader's toxicity are "hidden poisons" that must be addressed with as much earnestness as the more apparent behaviors. The following are examples leaders who displays hidden poisons.

- They draw conclusions without listening.
- They focus on attacking and blaming.
- They hinder promotions or other opportunities for visibility, due to jealousy or lack of self-confidence.
- They provide no feedback for improvement, but continue to say "all is fine," while silently planning your demise, or your exit out of the organization.
- They say one thing but do something else. [3]

Now, let's move our attention to strategies we can use to work with a toxic leader. Although dealing with their toxicity can be draining, it is critical to stay positive and avoid bitterness. Doing so will also help you remove your emotions from the situation. Stay away from communication wars that include email and verbal conflict. Next, you have to maintain your assertiveness so that you do not lose sight of your boundaries and values. Consider that when you stay silent, you are contributing to the toxic environment by allowing it to continue; hence, you become an enabler. Also, attempt to have a conversation with the toxic leader, but be prepared for any response and "don't expect a person to change."[4]

Another important strategy is to communicate with other staff members, which includes HR (more about that in the next insight) to help you with managing up when it comes to your leader. Rely on your village of supporters, and avoid isolating yourself in feelings of inadequacy and defeat.

A Black female executive shared some of her own experiences of being in a toxic work environment. Like many dedicated leaders, she believed if she simply put her head down and worked hard, that her work would stand on its own and prove that she "belonged" in her position. She quickly learned that this was not the right approach. After being in a culture in which she was not supported by her leader for a number of years, she had to learn how to survive by recognizing that her boss did not value her or have her best interests at heart. For example, this boss constantly took vacations because "she knew that I would handle the operations in her absence and all would be good. . . . I also had to learn that by sitting and saying 'woe is me' and 'this is not fair,' I would never make a change. I finally had to take back control, and truly prioritize other things such as my family and activities outside of work."

This executive also shared the importance of tapping into your network to help support you through precarious situations. Specifically, she commented that perhaps she would have made different decisions about how long she was willing to stay at that organization and with that leader had she used her own network to her advantage.

She recognized why it's so important to keep your résumé updated. "You don't want to be in a situation where you are thinking about leaving, and it adds another layer of stress and overwhelm when you are trying to dig through to recall project work, tasks, and accomplishments. . . . Especially if you are in a toxic situation, you are not always thinking clearly. For us as Black leaders, stress and overwhelm have tremendous consequences on our health and well-being, and it is easy to think we will just work through it. If you are a talented leader and have skills, you owe yourself more than to be in an environment where you have to deal with toxic workplaces or toxic bosses."

x— Insight 26 → o

Prevail Over Blackballing, Favoritism, and Unbearable Work Environments

The phenomenon of *blackballing*, which can be defined as ostracizing or excluding someone, or offering an adverse vote against someone that disables them from membership in an organization, is especially salient in the discussion of toxic cultures. Blackballing has particular relevance to the experiences of many BIPOC leaders and is often seen as a dark and dangerous act. For example, when a person is being considered for joining a team, regardless of how many people vote yes, a single no from an anonymous person can reject the candidate. What makes this dangerous is that the rule can neither be avoided nor renewed. Blackballing is usually done in extreme confidentiality. It also may be at play when a highly qualified employee applies for a job and is repeatedly met with radio silence.

A Black female healthcare executive I spoke with shared an experience of being the only African American woman in a senior leadership role within her organization. "I thought when I went to work for this team that my leader was progressive. . . . I later discovered that she was really all about herself, and I was hired because of my reputation for being a very hard worker with sound operational skills. To my face, she said, 'You're a great employee,' but she didn't really develop me for the next level. Here I was, working double and triple time, yet I wasn't being readied for other opportunities to advance."

This executive was literally blocked from being promoted internally, not because she wasn't worthy of a promotion but because her direct leader recognized that she was too valuable to let go. "I knew I was being blocked from advancing within the company when I had interviewed several times for opportunities and wasn't getting any of them. And as I asked for feedback, I came to find out that there was 'no reason' that could explain why I wasn't getting any callbacks with offers. Even though I consistently received good performance evaluations, sadly it became clear I was never going to advance under her leadership. I don't think she ever said anything outrightly negative when others called her to ask about me, but she certainly never shared the type of feedback that would have *helped* my chances of being selected. I finally had to come to the realization that no matter how hard I worked, I was never going to advance within that company." Ultimately, this leader chose to leave the organization altogether. When I asked her about her experiences with this leader and the organization, she absolutely felt like she was blackballed.

Blackballing is often accompanied by favoritism. When you are on the other end of favoritism, this can work for you in the short or even the long term. However, it can be hell when you are not one of the favorites on the team. I have learned the hard way that no matter the organization, there will undoubtedly be a leader who displays favoritism, whether intentionally or unintentionally. The most toxic form of this is when the leader intentionally creates an unbearable work environment by not treating an individual with dignity and respect. They might use their influence and positional power to turn other leaders against you, or intentionally exclude you from projects. They will likely offer preferential treatment to others that extends to access to promotional opportunities.

In considering unbearable work environments, I am reminded of a recent conversation I had with a senior executive who shared a gem that has stuck with me to this day: "Life is too short for you to work for and with people that you don't like or respect." He told me this in response to my asking him about managing some internal politics, specifically about how to work with particularly challenging personalities. I was in a relatively new role at that point, and he offered the support and advice I needed at the time. He went on to share that there are two types of leaders in the workplace. The first will tolerate negativity and toxicity because they are unwilling to change their surroundings—for a variety of reasons. Perhaps they don't want to explore the unknown or go into what may be a different role or organization and have to deal with the same things. Perhaps they are not courageous enough to take a risk. Some may capitulate to poor treatment because they feel that's just their lot in life. (I am here to say that it is *not*.)

The second type of leader is one who decides to take the risk and make different career choices because life is too short to tolerate an intolerable situation. The important point here is: once you identify the toxicity, you have the power to do something about it, even if it means removing yourself from the environment. I am sure you have heard time and again that you do not and should not have to stay in a workplace that merely *tolerates* you.

It is unfortunate to note the number of leaders of color with whom I have spoken who, at some point in their careers, experienced toxicity in the workplace. If you count yourself among them, my heart goes out to you. If you have been able to climb the ladder and achieve all your goals and dreams with absolutely no politics or toxicity, hats off to you!

Another Black executive shared the importance of "staying true to yourself and digging to ask honest questions about where you are and where you want to be. One of the most important aspects of any role is the relationship I will have with my boss. I don't want to be miserable every day because I am working with a leader who doesn't support or value me. I had to learn the hard way to not give anyone else control of my joy, my power, or my energy."

For many leaders of color, who may be the victims of conscious and unconscious bias alike, it is crucial to learn how to manage favoritism, as frustrating and unfair as it can be. At some point in your career, you will likely encounter a leader who plays favorites. If not, count your blessings! The worst thing you can do if you are in an intolerable work environment is nothing. Even if you fear retribution, know that you are a descendant of kings and queens! In the wise words of Mary McLeod Bethune, "If we have the courage and tenacity of our forebears, who stood firmly like a rock against the lash of slavery, we shall find a way to do for our day what they did for theirs."[5]

Here are some steps you can take if you feel that you are in a hostile or toxic work environment.

- **Document actions.** If you truly want to find a resolution, it is important to demonstrate examples of how the leader has shown you hostility.
- **Be open and transparent.** During any conversation about how you've been treated—whether you've encountered a toxic boss, blackballing, favoritism, or anything else—set the stage for your conversation in a tone that is collaborative instead of defensive. If you are in a hostile environment, regardless of what you do, your tone might be perceived as angry or aggressive; you must stay calm and collected, but stand your ground.

- **Reach out to others.** If having a crucial conversation with your leader does not resolve the issue, it is important to reach out discreetly to another ally who can support you. I recommend reaching out to your HR representative for a confidential conversation for advice and guidance to help you be successful.

- **Invest in your emotional health and wellness.** No matter what, your emotional wellness should not be compromised in order for you to remain where you are. Again, everyone makes choices about how they want to be treated; in the end, don't let your mental health suffer because of a role, leader, or an organization.

- **Offer your leader the benefit of the doubt.** I know what you're thinking here: a toxic leader *knows* they are being toxic! If there is a snowball's chance in hell that maybe, just maybe, the individual has zero self-awareness and no perception of how they are coming across to others, extend the benefit of the doubt—but only once! Trust your gut and use common sense. You know when you are being disrespected and demeaned.

More than any other topic I've written about in this book, managing workplace politics and toxic cultures has become a recurring theme for so many leaders of color. It is crushing to know what these more-than-capable and uber-talented individuals have had to endure. This is why I am so passionate about assisting others in excelling in the face of the heavy burden of a toxic work environment. Learning how to navigate especially challenging people and situations is a muscle that you will very likely use at some point in your career—and it's not a matter of if but when.

"Caring for myself is not self-indulgence, it is self-preservation, and that is an act of political warfare."

—Audre Lorde, writer, civil-rights activist

CHAPTER 12

Prioritizing Your Emotional Well-Being and Finding Work-Life Integration

*I*f it isn't already obvious, a good leader is instrumental in promoting the well-being of their team members, but all too often, they might forget to treat themselves with the same level of care. As a leader, you are carrying the weight of many important decisions, not to mention other people's livelihoods. Given the responsibilities that you hold, it is critical to maintain the vessel of your body, mind, and spirit in a way that promotes clarity and preserves your energy. Having a lifestyle that is already positive—including a healthy diet, adequate sleep, and regular exercise—builds a foundation for maximizing the flow of positive emotions. This solid foundation equips you with the fuel necessary for coping with significant events, including major changes in your organization or potential setbacks in your business.

There have been countless studies on what it means to achieve a balance between work and life. But the idea of *work-life balance* has forced many people to judge themselves about showing emotion at work, after all, we all have heard the mandate to "leave your emotions at the door." However, balance isn't about compartmentalizing and excluding our lived experiences from our nine-to-five jobs. To be integrated human beings is to have the freedom to bring all parts of ourselves to every aspect of our lives. This is why I prefer the term *work-life integration.*

Work-life integration is crucial to total well-being, and it begins with doing work that is fulfilling and meaningful to you. Even though this chapter does not detail the intricacies of doing work you enjoy, I want to note that your work and life should not battle each other; they should be aligned. Even if you are not particularly fond of your current occupation, you'll find helpful information here.

To be clear, work-life integration is not one-size-fits-all and looks different for everyone. Ultimately, it is about honoring how you have committed to spend your time. Each method that follows can be tweaked and adjusted as you see fit, and applies both to you and your team members. Leaders have to be willing to assist their teams in work-life integration by offering practices to help them avoid burnout. But before you can do that for your team, you must be able to utilize balancing practices within your own work and life.

- **Schedule your break times.** If you know you can work two hours straight without taking a break, then do so; but be deliberate about your break and honor that time and yourself!
- **Build in your vacations.** Create space in your calendar for a break. Be intentional about unplugging and rejuvenating your mind and body so that you can be productive and fresh to create, innovate, and execute ideas.
- **Recognize what you are spending time on.** Identifying how you spend your time could be as simple as deciding what you do and don't like to do. This can help you do tasks that are most fulfilling, then outsource or delegate the others. This process can help you determine if you are

doing a job you might be good at or recognize whether someone else would be better at it.

- **Recognize if you tend to fill up your entire day.** When you have reached your peak point, don't look for the next project! Also, take the opportunity to enjoy any free time that has opened up before committing to something else or setting out to achieve another goal.

- **Stop being hard on yourself.** Many leaders are overly hard on themselves; working mothers, especially, may have a tendency to experience "mommy guilt" when it comes to the time we must spend on work. If you know you have a big project approaching with a deadline in the next thirty days, you may only be able to eat dinner with your children three nights out of the week. The joy is setting the expectation and knowing that the adjustment is only temporary.

- **Make choices to get your life back under your control.** You can manage your preferences and decide on the outcomes that you want. This might require making decisions that challenge other people's assumptions and routines—such as starting your workday early or ending early because you want to spend time with your kids or on a hobby outside of work.

- **Ask for support.** Remember to lean on your network in and out of the workplace. Muster the courage to make unconventional requests. For example, perhaps an adjusted schedule like the one mentioned above will allow you to manage your life better. Or perhaps you can ask for a hybrid schedule that will enable you to come into the office three days a week and work remotely the other two.

As a leader, you wear many hats. But this does not mean being everything to everybody. While this applies to male and female leaders, it's important to highlight here the challenges women leaders face. According to the Mayo Clinic, women are "twice as likely as men to be diagnosed with depression."[1] This may be compounded by the fact that women generally have a more challenging time saying no. When you are creating balance, you are opening time for completing projects that you are passionate about. Saying no invites space for having an outlet. If you work from home, it is essential not to feel guilty for refusing to accept another project or saying no to staying online for two extra hours. Saying no also applies to invitations outside the workplace from your circle of family and friends. Make it clear that just because you work from home, this does not mean you have increased availability.

In her book *Becoming*, former first lady Michelle Obama writes about her transition back into full-time employment after having her second child. She accepted the role of a hospital executive while raising two children. She felt as though the weight of the world was on her shoulders due to her husband's political schedule. She lost time working out, was not as healthy as she wanted to be, and was unable to eat dinner with her family consistently. In her attempt to gain balance, Mrs. Obama's focus words (words that serve as overarching reminders of a goal one wishes to achieve, which can be powerful in guiding intention and attention) became *strength* and *calm*. She set boundaries within her family. She ate dinner with her children at the same time each day, whether her husband was home or not. She enlisted the help of her mother to dedicate time in the morning to working out. Her focus words allowed her to find balance—and more importantly, integration.[2]

x— Insight 27 → o

Prevent Burnout

Another aspect of work-life integration is managing stress, which impacts our physical and mental health and behaviors. Let's look briefly at the physical symptoms of stress: increased heart rate, sweating, muscle pain, and headaches, among others. Often, when a specific behavior affects our physical bodies, we begin to understand that behavior's impacts. However, the behaviors we engage in as a result of stress are not always as noticeable. They might look like making hasty decisions, being disengaged and isolated from peers, and emphasizing worry and fear over inspiration.

Ignoring stress and its consequences can easily lead to burnout, which can be defined as "a state of emotional, mental, and often physical exhaustion brought on by prolonged or repeated stress."[3] The causes of burnout will vary from person to person, but they include perfectionism and attempting to do too much on your own by telling yourself things like, "I should be able to do this by myself. I'm good at it!" The causes of burnout specific to the workplace include overwork, lack of cohesion among leadership, invisible leadership, and staff shortage, to name a few.

In March 2020, the COVID-19 pandemic ravaged the world, and in 2021, the great resignation took place, during which scores of women and men left their roles and organizations, or their careers altogether, for a variety of reasons, but mostly due to burnout, fatigue, and stress, as well as the promise of more opportunities for flexibility and greater balance elsewhere. Data from several organizations, including think tanks and tech firms, have noted that burnout (which has been partially associated with having a toxic leader or work environment, as we discussed in the previous chapter) is one of the biggest reasons people are leaving their jobs. Cengage Group, a global education tech firm, conducted a poll in late November 2021 among 1,200 US workers who had recently resigned or planned to within the next six months. According to the poll, 89 percent of people reported feeling burnt out and unsupported, and 82 percent noted that the pandemic had forced them to reconsider their priorities—all factors that offer employers a vital opportunity to think about what they're doing to support their team members' mental health and professional growth.[4]

The great resignation may have been a blessing in disguise because it actually began fueling creative and even innovative workplace approaches to retaining the best and most talented workers. Mental health and wellness needs to be of the utmost importance when organizations are creating strategies to retain their employees. It is essential for both individuals and companies to recognize burnout in the early stages, because, if prolonged, it leads to more intense emotional problems, such as depression. We know the detrimental effects of long-term depression (a topic that goes beyond the scope of this book).

The signs of burnout can be subtle and are often overlooked. The following is a brief list of symptoms as shared by Terri Ferguson, LCSW, therapist, mindset coach, and founder of Solution Savvy Counseling and Training. You may have experienced any or all of these symptoms at one time or another:

- inability to focus
- inability to sleep
- lack of motivation
- irritability
- physical and mental exhaustion
- isolating from peers

- exhaustion
- lack of joy and enthusiasm[5]

So, how do we manage our stress and eliminate burnout when faced with an extreme change of events and deadlines? It is always helpful to create a plan. Consider how you can adjust your routine. This might include incorporating relaxation techniques into your life and identifying how you can rely on your support system even more. Remember, you can always return to your previous routine or keep your new plan, as you may find that your adjusted routine fits into your life even under normal circumstances.

To avoid burnout, it is OK and encouraged to step away from a situation to prevent responding inappropriately or taking on too much. Prepare to handle the situation by reassuring yourself that you have what it takes to do so. Referring to the list of symptoms can be helpful with identifying triggers that signal you are entering burnout mode. For a few days, take note of events, conversations, or information received that caused you the most unease in mind and body. Write down how you responded: write the first thought that entered your mind and how you reacted physically. If you have experienced burnout before, this will be easy, because you probably already know your triggers. This technique will help you in the midst of a challenging time and will enable you to get ahead of burnout. I would be remiss if I did not emphasize that you do not have to handle stress and burnout alone. Please do not be ashamed to seek professional therapy.

Leaders need to understand that stress levels vary among people, because we all perceive and experience situations differently. However, when you have recognized the stress symptoms and early stages of burnout in yourself, it is easy to identify them in others. It will also qualify you to provide tools for stress relief to your team, because you have utilized them yourself.

You may notice a team member is having difficulty working on a task. The problem does not stem from lack of ability, but you see that they are allowing fear to drive their behavior. As a leader, let them know that you are available to help. Offer to work on the project with them, or consider removing some of their responsibilities for a certain amount of time to allow them to regain their footing. During this time, plan a conversation to understand the basis of their fear better. It could be that this one conversation is exactly what the person needs to resume their work with confidence. Most importantly, remind your team members that they do not have to cope with stress and burnout alone. If you work in an organization that provides employee assistance programs, gently remind them that help is available.

x— Insight 28 → o

Gain Resilience and Respond to What Life Throws at You

Resilience can be defined as the ability to recover quickly from setbacks. It is the kind of toughness that allows a person to spring back to their original state without a prolonged recovery time. Resilience is often seen as a superpower and treated like a trait that not everyone possesses, but it is indeed something that can be cultivated.

If you wish to become an integral part of a leadership team and resilience does not seem to flow to you naturally, you can certainly seek training to make it one of your intrinsic qualities. Of course, resilience is usually not necessary on the days when everything is going as perfectly planned, but it is paramount when nothing is going your way due to unforeseen circumstances.

Let us not confuse resilience with ignoring and wishing emotions away. It requires facing uncomfortable situations head-on.

Resilient leaders tend to encourage even more communication and collaboration. A leader knows that during times of extreme change, they must not turn away from their team or attempt to "go it alone" by independently doing all the planning, goal setting, and decision-making, without team members' assistance or input. This can add even more stress to an already stressful situation, as it undermines your team members' agency and autonomy.

In chapter 7, I highlighted an interview with Cathy Hughes and her suggestion for leaders to take the time to think through their decisions. Doing so is vital for you as a leader because it will give you space for a personal mental check-in before you check in on everyone else's well-being.

Not everyone welcomes change or uncertainty, so they will depend on leaders for guidance. They even look to us to notice how we respond to unfavorable situations. When we take our influence seriously, we are more mindful of our responses and how we communicate processes to accommodate changes. A resilient leader will always work to cultivate a greater level of togetherness. Even amid chaos, an intense focus on togetherness can provide the kind of camaraderie that will lead to solace and increased support. People will be confident in expressing their feelings without fear of being judged or perceived as overly emotional.

Resilient leaders know how to balance the current reality against the awareness that there is a better tomorrow in sight—even when it may not necessarily feel that way. They move through difficult situations with courage and persistence, which is an indicator of emotional intelligence.

If you are resilient, you recognize that there will be challenges on the path to achieving a goal, and despite how difficult it may be, it's worth pushing through your own self-sabotage and preconceived limitations. Building resilience rests on the foundation of understanding that true success is in the effort you put in versus what the results might be. The results will come as long as the effort is there, but the effort must be consistent and unwavering.

How is it that one group of leaders is able to navigate seemingly insurmountable struggles without much trouble, while others crumble in the face of those very same challenges? Psychologist and author Angela Duckworth characterizes those who have grit as being resilient, hardworking, and in possession of a combination of passion and perseverance.[6]

A great example of why resilience is important in the workplace can be found at the postgraduate level. Many graduate students are led to believe they'll receive appropriate training from their employers, but enter the workplace without any prior knowledge and must face countless obstacles on the path to mastery. Many careers require adaptability as well as the ability to learn a new skill quickly. If an employee doesn't have what it takes, it's likely that they will feel overwhelmed by the challenge and give up before learning the skill.[7]

I've discussed the matter of how to build resilience with a number of leaders of color, and I've realized how it looks from individual to individual. For therapist and mindset coach Terri Ferguson, who works with her clients to help them develop greater resilience and follow-through, resilience is "based on the real relationships you have with yourself and with your faith, as well as with others in your support system. It's important to have a few key people that you trust, who accept you unconditionally, so that when you need the support or push, you have people around you that you can rely on."

When I spoke with Ferguson, she noted that she has had many conversations with high-achieving executives of color who were raised with the understanding that life is "unfair" and that they will have to work twice as hard to get half the recognition. At the same time, she notes, "I also feel we have to learn boundaries. Even in high-stress, high-pressure, high-demand jobs where the odds are already stacked against you, it is important to strike a balance. Many people struggle with this mental trap. I call it a *trap* because no one can reasonably meet some of these expectations of never taking time away until you're so depleted and exhausted, your body forces you to do so. When you establish patterns of behavior for yourself, what you're also doing is establishing or determining what others will expect of you and from you. . . . You have to do your craft with excellence, but don't be so overwhelmed by it all that you lose out on the self-care . . . for the sake of trying to climb the ladder."[8]

Ferguson has seen a growing trend of people choosing to stand up for their values, families, and personal space—and it begins with recognizing their own self-worth. She recommends two major ways to cultivate resilience through greater self-care:

1. **Listen to your body.** "You can only go so long without rest, food, and water. You can only go for so long until your ability to take in information decreases. It's like climbing a mountain: you peak, and then there's this decline. Listen to your body. If you need to stretch, go stretch."
2. **Take a break.** "So as we're working, it's still the same thing. . . . We need a break, even if it's just five or ten minutes to shift to something else so that we can recuperate and then go back to it. . . . Look outside, walk down the stairs, get some water, go interact with somebody for a couple of minutes, and then come back to your activity. We need those kinds of deliberate pauses throughout the day to keep our momentum."[9]

A Black male hospital executive I spoke with reiterated the power and importance of self-care in establishing resilience and also offered that there is enormous value in identifying and aligning with one's priorities, which can help develop the boundaries that Ferguson deemed so important. This leader shared, "At some point, you have to be in the right state of mind to function, and sometimes that means stepping away. Also, you have to ask yourself what is important, and specifically, what are your priorities. For me, it is easier to step away now because I have made significant sacrifices in my jobs at various times. I know that my family is important, and I want my kids to have memories of me being engaged and present with them and not working all the time. It doesn't mean I will not give my all, but I have to balance. . . . So, am I going to continue to work hard? Yes. However, I am not afraid to take two weeks' vacation and just disappear or take a long weekend, because I need it, and my family needs it."

As many leaders of color have learned, grit, devotion, and dedication can only work for us to a point. Caring for ourselves in body, mind, and spirit is one of the fastest paths to gaining resilience and the deeper conviction that allows us to commit to being the leaders we are for the long haul.

Beautiful has always been our Black

Be it on the Motherland

or across the diaspora

Our very existence is

Strength

Resilience

Perseverance

My spirit

The Cradle of civilization

Mother of creation

Alkebu-lan greatness

Embedded in every bit of our melanin

—Ross Cooper, poet and creative writer

CONCLUSION

The journey has only just begun.

My mission to help amplify the voices of Black leaders (and by extension, other BIPOC leaders) in corporate spaces has been the driving force fueling this piece of leadership equity work. My own journey in the corporate world was filled with optimism, visibility, and opportunities, but also some disappointment, despair, frustration, and even pain. However, I remain hopeful that, through this book, I am helping to share my own point of view and the perspectives of other leaders on topics that continue to keep so many Black professionals from achieving the career trajectories that their experience and background deserve.

I am reminded that Black people have come a long way since our forefathers and foremothers stepped foot on this land hundreds of years ago. However, as recent world events have shown, we have further to go to achieve equity and parity in so many areas, including in corporate leadership and executive roles.

As I write this, we are in the midst of the great resignation, and more and more people are making the decision to no longer remain in their current organizations; they are choosing to move to other organizations or leave corporate altogether. For those who want to stay and do their best work, the tools, tips, and resources to not only survive but thrive are outlined here for the taking.

As much as I had painstakingly planned the intricate steps of my career and life story, the journey was not easy. Some days, I wish I had chosen an easier path to my career goals. However, I recall the biblical words: "To whom much is given, much will be required." And I have been given so much. People invested in me early in my career. Now, I want to impact leaders globally; it is my time. I am also reminded that my experiences can help others, and as much as I can share what I learned so that someone else will not have to endure certain heartaches, then it will not have been in vain.

My hope is that, in the process of reading this book, you will have learned from the emotional ups and downs as well as the achievements of others I have highlighted. As we continue to climb the corporate ladder, our experiences don't occur in a vacuum, and these stories showcase that we all are dealing with similar issues and challenges, regardless of industry or environment. That's why it is important for us to bond together and support each other as we climb! For future generations of leaders who are optimistic about what corporate life is like, I encourage you to continue to be bold and brave and go about your journey of achievement with all of the fierceness you can muster. The spirit of our ancestors is with us— they are watching and celebrating our collective successes.

As I've been putting the final touches on this book, my own career and life journey have shifted. In my introduction, you learned that I spent more than fifteen years in the C-suite within the hospital and healthcare industry. In the summer of 2021, I walked away from corporate America and took some much-needed time to reconnect with my family, who had lost me for a while as I was dealing with my own internal and external struggles. I now have the opportunity to delve into a variety of interests and passions that I heretofore felt uncomfortable exploring fully. Finally, I am now at that fabled fork in the road: as much as I enjoyed the lifestyle, skills, and relationships that will last me two lifetimes, the time has come for me to enjoy my calling to help amplify the voices and capabilities of other leaders who look like me, and do so under my own company and brand.

Between the summers of 2020 and 2021, as the world was still reeling from the impacts of COVID-19 and social and civil unrest, I was dealing with my own reawakening and finally felt the confidence and courage to pursue my calling on my own terms. I am grateful and thankful for the support of family and friends who didn't bat an eye when I shared what I wanted to do. I continue to be amazed at the outpouring of support from those near and far as I share my own journey and experiences—the good, the bad, and the ugly—to help others.

I also encourage anyone who may be struggling in toxic environments, with toxic leaders, or in roles in which they are ill-suited, to not waste any more time pondering what to do. Make an exit plan! There are too many opportunities available for talented leaders to endure misery, especially now. There are cultures and organizations that will value your expertise through a lens of cultural appreciation, so do not wait for things to get better. Your emotional and mental health and wellness depend on it, and you owe it to yourself to seek more.

Here's my call to action for you: As you are climbing the career ladder and experiencing success beyond all measure, grab the hand of someone else and pull them along. Open the doors for others. Pull a chair up to the table for those behind you. I certainly was not able to achieve the success I wanted without others opening the doors of opportunity for me.

If you are an ally reading this book, I hope you have been inspired to be a change agent to help bring about new opportunities for leaders of color who are smart, intelligent, and talented—leaders who deserve more than what they are currently receiving. Don't just check the diversity and inclusion boxes without doing the work it takes to usher in a new host of leaders who are truly reflective of the communities in which we live and work. I invite you to join in and support colleagues, friends, and family who are still in corporate environments. Be supportive, offer mentorship and sponsorship opportunities and any other chances for the talented to rise and have a seat, as well as a meaningful voice, at the table.

As I end this book, I share the inspirational words from the poem "Mother to Son," by Langston Hughes.

> *Well, son, I'll tell you:*
> *Life for me ain't been no crystal stair.*
> *It's had tacks in it,*
> *And splinters,*
> *And boards torn up,*
> *And places with no carpet on the floor—*
> *Bare.*

I hope when my own son reads this book one day, he will know that his mommy took the tacks and splinters and boards and created her own story fueled by a desire for better—for this generation, and the next, and the next—and that she did it her way.

I hope you have enjoyed reading this as much as I enjoyed writing it!

To stay up to date, visit my website at unwritteninsights.com and join me as we support transformational leaders of color around the world.

Yours in leadership,
Lenetra

ACKNOWLEDGMENTS

Where do I begin?

I am so very blessed and fortunate to have a list of people to thank for helping me get this book into the world. Thank you God Almighty for giving me more abundant life and the courage to pursue my passions. My path looks very different now from what I had envisioned and long worked toward. Through faith and perseverance, I will continue to be steadfast in chasing big and bold dreams that keep me on that path to share my story, experiences, insights, and perspectives to help others and the next generation of leaders coming behind me.

I am thankful for my entire family of course. To my husband who stood frequently in the gap at home so I could focus on this project, thank you for your love and patience. To my son—I missed many nights of snuggle time so I could finish this book. One day, I hope you read it and understand that my sacrifice was to ensure you are afforded all the opportunities you deserve, and then some. To my mom, Great Uncle James, my cousins Angela and Lolita, and Aunt Cheryl—there is not enough space in this book for me to share how much I appreciate your always being there for me, no questions asked.

I am surrounded by many talented, remarkable, and exceptional women—thank you for who you are to me and all you do for those around you. I am grateful for your years of support, friendship, prayers, love, memories, and everything in between: Ohme Entin, Stephanie Griffith, Lori Thomas-Gray, Kamara White, LaToya Hunt, LoriAnn Lypson, Crystal Brown, Jeane Holmes, Lisa Odom, and Daphney Young.

I have many colleagues, mentors, and sponsors who opened

doors, created access to opportunities, gave me advice when I didn't know which way to go, poured into me, and helped to shape me into the leader I am today. I am especially thankful to Antionette Smith Epps, Deborah Lee Eddie, Dell Oliver, and Dr. Bob Lynch for having learned from you. I will continue to use my voice as a platform to mentor the next generation. I am even grateful for observing and experiencing less than "leaderly" traits from individuals whose characteristics taught me valuable lessons about what not to replicate!

To all the Black leaders who spent hours on Zoom meetings, phone calls, and answering my emails, I applaud you from the bottom of my heart for your transparency and your willingness to support me. Not a single one of you hesitated when asked if you would be part of this effort—your stories are powerful, and your leadership is commendable. You know who you are, and I am forever grateful!

To my editorial team, Nirmala Nataraj and Elisabeth Rinaldi, who went back and forth with me for months on this manuscript (smile)—you both had the unenviable job of getting my ideas and content organized, focused, and clear. Many thanks for your patience and stellar service standards. A huge shout out and note of thanks to Kumisha Saffold for connecting me with Ross Cooper, whose poetic prowess shined through for this project.

Thank you to those who have played any part in my career, business ventures, or in this book coming to fruition. And I am grateful in advance for individuals who will support me by reading and sharing. My desire is that leaders of color and allies will use what you learned in this book to facilitate true transformation in your organizations and for your own life and career. I look forward to hearing from you about what your next chapter brings!

ABOUT THE AUTHOR

*L*enetra King is founder and CEO of Watch Me EXCEL®, a leadership development firm that works in a pioneering way with organizations to deeply engage, promote, and retain exceptional leaders, especially those from underrepresented populations. Using her more than fifteen years of experience as a hospital C-Suite executive, Lenetra's passion for driving results in employee engagement and workforce culture, patient and consumer experience, quality, operational excellence, and financial performance all come to bear in the various pathways in which she works with clients.

Lenetra is a nationally sought-after speaker on navigating workplace politics and leveraging sponsorship for career and leadership success in the workplace. As a Black executive, it was important to Lenetra to take the leadership lessons she learned and observed and share them with others, especially leaders of color trying to figure out the maze of career advancement in corporate environments.

Her community-trustee interests include healthcare equity

and the elimination of racial disparities, mental health access, social justice, youth development and education. She has volunteered for close to thirty different nonprofit organizations over the course of her adult life and is a member of Delta Sigma Theta Sorority, Inc. A passionate advocate of historically Black colleges and universities, Lenetra currently serves on the Florida A&M University Foundation board of directors.

She received a bachelor of science degree from Florida A&M University, a master of science in health administration from the University of Alabama at Birmingham, and a master of business administration from Rockhurst University.

To connect with Lenetra, please visit www.unwritteninsights. com.

ENDNOTES

Introduction

1. Jeanne Sahadi, June 2, 2020, "After years of talking about diversity, the number of black leaders at US companies is still dismal," *CNN Business*, https://www.cnn.com/2020/06/02/success/diversity-and-black-leadership-in-corporate-america/index.html

2. Lindsay Kaplan, March 1, 2022, "This Women's History Month, here's a radical idea: Let women lead," *Fortune*, https://fortune.com/2022/03/01/it-is-past-time-for-women-to-lead/

Chapter 1

1. Maria Rosario T. de Guzman, Tonia R. Durden, et al., "Cultural Competence: An Important Skill Set for the 21st Century, NebGuide, G1375 · Index: Youth & Families, Families, Issued February 2016, https://extensionpublications.unl.edu/assets/html/g1375/build/g1375.htm

2. Georgetown University, "Definitions of cultural competence," Curricula Enhancement Module Series, https://nccc.georgetown.edu/curricula/culturalcompetence.html

3. Ibid.

Chapter 2

1. Dictionary.com, Definition of "implicit bias," https://www.dictionary.com/browse/implicit-bias

2. Perception Institute, "Implicit Bias," https://perception.org/research/implicit-bias

3. Harvard University's diagnostic tools around implicit bias are especially helpful and only get to the tip of the iceberg when it comes to helping people gain awareness of their unconscious attitudes, https://implicit.harvard.edu/implicit/takeatest.html

4. Bureau of Labor Statistics, April 2021, *Women in the labor force: A databook*, https://www.bls.gov/opub/reports/womens-databook/2020/home.htm#:~:text=In%202019%2C%2057.4%20percent%20of,of%2060.0%20percent%20in%201999

5. Katharina Buchholz, "Only 8 Percent of CEOs at Fortune 500 Companies Are Female," Statista, June 4, 2021, https://www.statista.com/chart/13995/female-ceos-in-fortune-500-companies/#:~:text=2021%20is%20seeing%20a%20new,the%20country's%20biggest%20public%20businesses

6. Kim Elsesser, "6 Dismal Findings from U.N. Report on Gender Bias," *Forbes*, March 9, 2020.

7. Ibid.

8. Amarette Filut, Anna Kaatz, and Molly Carnes, *The Impact of Unconscious Bias on Women's Career Advancement*, The Sasakawa Peace Foundation Expert Reviews Series on Advancing Women's Empowerment, 2017. https://www.spf.org/publication/upload/Unconscious%20Bias%20and%20Womens%20Careers_2017_en.pdf

9. Neighborhood House, "The harmful impacts of implicit bias and systemic racism," http://neighb.org/harmful-impacts-implicit-bias-systemic-racism/

10. Glenn Jeffers, "Want to retain your diverse workforce? Focus on removing bias," *Talent Management*, September 2, 2020, https://www.vistage.com/research-center/talent-management/20200902-remove-unconscious-bias/

11. Enumale Agada, "Sidney Poitier, Mike Brown, and the Myth of Black Exceptionalism," *Celluloid in Black and White* (blog), January 11, 2015, http://celluloidinblackandwhite.blogspot.com/2015/01/sidney-poitier-mike-brown-and-myth-of.html

12. Rosalie Chamberlain, *Conscious Leadership in the Workplace: A Guidebook to Making a Difference One Person at a Time*, (New York, NY: Morgan James Publishing, 2016)

13. Free Dictionary, Definition of "microaggression," https://www.thefreedictionary.com/microaggression

14. Dr. Phil McGraw, "How You May Be Using Microaggressions Without Being Aware of It," YouTube, October 18, 2018, https://www.youtube.com/watch?v=9bqtfRKZkRE

15. Tiffany Alvoid, "Eliminating Microaggressions: The Next Level of

Inclusion," TEDx Oakland, December 9, 2019, https://www.youtube.com/watch?v=cPqVit6TJjw

16. Dr. Joy Bradford, "Understanding Racial Microaggression and Its Impact on Mental Health," Pfizer. https://www.pfizer.com/news/hot-topics/understanding_racial_microaggression_and_its_effect_on_mental_health

17. Robert T. Carter, "Racism and Psychological and Emotional Injury: Recognizing and Assessing Race-Based Traumatic Stress," *The Counseling Psychologist*, January 2007.

18. Ariane Resnick, "What Is Racial Trauma?" Very Well Mind, November 30, 2021, https://www.verywellmind.com/what-is-racial-trauma-5210344

19. Border Crossers, "What Is Unconscious Bias? What Are Microaggressions?" https://nfty.org/wp-content/uploads/sites/32/2017/02/3-Definitions-of-UB-and-MA.pdf

20. William F. Martin, "Minority Mental Health: The Syndemic Leaders Can't Ignore," American College of Healthcare Executives, https://www.ache.org/blog/2021/minority-mental-health-the-syndemic-leaders-cant-ignore

21. Ibid.

22. D. Fekedulegn, Toni Alterman, et al., "Prevalence of Workplace Discrimination and Mistreatment in a National Sample of Older US Workers: The REGARDS Cohort Study," *SSM - Population Health, vol. 8, 100444*, (2019).

23. Derek R. Avery and Enrica N. Ruggs, "Confronting the Uncomfortable Reality of Workplace Discrimination," *Sloan Review*, July 14, 2020, https://sloanreview.mit.edu/article/confronting-the-uncomfortable-reality-of-workplace-discrimination/

24. Elma Mrkonjic, "43 Troubling Employment Discrimination Statistics for 2021," *The High Court*, July 4, 2021.

25. Ibid.

26. Ibid.

27. Ibid.

28. Earl Fitzhugh, JP Julien, Nick Noel, and Shelley Stewart, "It's time for a new approach to racial equity," McKinsey and Company, December 2, 2020, https://www.mckinsey.com/featured-insights/diversity-and-inclusion/its-time-for-a-new-approach-to-racial-equity

29. Pooja Jain-Link, et al., "5 Strategies for Creating an Inclusive Workplace," *Harvard Business Review*, January 13, 2020, https://hbr.org/2020/01/5-strategies-for-creating-an-inclusive-workplace

30. US Census Bureau, "The Nation's Older Population Is Still Growing," June 22, 2017, https://www.census.gov/newsroom/press-releases/2017/cb17-100.html

Chapter 3

1. Dictionary.com, Definition of "mindset," https://www.dictionary.com/browse/mindset

2. Kamlesh Singh, "Positive Psychology," http://www.nitttrc.edu.in/nptel/courses/video/109102157/lec2.pdf, Accessed June 29, 2022.

3. Ibid.

4. Amy Cuddy, *Presence: Bringing Your Boldest Self to Your Biggest Challenges*, (New York: Hachette Book Group, 2015), 45–46.

5. Tara Mohr, "Playing Big: Find Your Voice, Your Mission, Your Message," *Talks at Google*, September 21, 2016, https://youtu.be/my7hIjQJRG4

6. Ibid.

7. You can find the CliftonStrengths assessment test on the Gallup website at https://www.gallup.com/cliftonstrengths/en/252137/home.aspx

8. Michael Hyatt, "How To Be a More Energetic Leader: 5 Things You Can Do Today to Regain Stamina and Enthusiasm," MichaelHyatt.com, https://michaelhyatt.com/how-to-be-a-more-energetic-leader/

Chapter 4

1. Nick Wolny, "What Jeff Bezos' Smart Take on Personal Branding Can Teach You About the Importance of Thought Leadership," Entrepreneur, August 24, 2021, https://www.entrepreneur.com/article/379920

2. Alison.com, "Introduction to Branding," https://alison.com/topic/learn/112735/introduction-to-branding

3. Ibid.

4. Ibid.

5. Nick Nelson (founder, The BRANDPRENUER Agency®), in discussion with the author, November 2021.

6. Michael Hyatt, *The Vision-Driven Leader: 10 Questions to Focus Your Efforts, Energize Your Team, and Scale Your Business*, (Michigan: Baker Publishing Group, 2020), 61.

7. Arnaud Chevallier, *Strategic Thinking in Problem Solving*, (New York, NY: Oxford University Press, 2016)

8. Denise Brosseau, *Ready to Be a Thought Leader?: How to Increase Your Influence, Impact, and Success*, (San Francisco, CA: Jossey-Bass, 2014)

9. "Sylvia Ann Hewlett," accessed April 26, 2022, https://www.sylviaannhewlett.com/about

10. Carol Cox (founder and CEO of Speaking Your Brand®), in discussion with the author, September 2021.

11. Carol Cox (founder and CEO of Speaking Your Brand®), in discussion with the author, September 2021.

12. Sylvia Ann Hewlett, *Executive Presence: The Missing Link Between Merit and Success*, (Kindle ebook version), (New York, NY: Harper Business, 2014), 5.

13. Sylvia Ann Hewlett, "Cracking the Code That Stalls People of Color," Harvard Business Review, January 22, 2014, https://hbr.org/2014/01/cracking-the-code-that-stalls-multicultural-professionals

14. Dove and Crown Coalition, The Crown Act, https://www.thecrownact.com

15. Ibid.

Chapter 5

1. P. Salovey & J.D. Mayer, 1990, "Emotional intelligence," *Imagination, Cognition, and Personality*, 9, 185–211

2. Daniel Goleman, "What Makes a Leader?" Harvard Business Review, January 2004, https://hbr.org/2004/01/what-makes-a-leader

3. Ibid.

4. Mitrefinch, "EQ (Emotional Intelligence) and the Future of Work," https://mitrefinch.com/blog/eq-future-work/

5. Travis Bradberry, August 26, 2021, "Emotional Intelligence Can Boost Your Career and Save Your Life," TalentSmartEQ, https://www.talentsmarteq.com/articles/Emotional-Intelligence-Can-Boost-Your-Career-And-Save-Your-Life-915340665-p-1.html/

6. Dinah Wisenberg Brin, November 1, 2013, "What Is Emotional Intelligence?" SHRM, https://www.shrm.org/resourcesandtools/hr-topics/behavioral-competencies/leadership-and-navigation/pages/what-is-emotional-intelligence.aspx

7. Anna Barber and Robyn Ward, December 28, 2020, "Survey Says: EQ for the Win in 2021 and Beyond," Medium, https://robynward.medium.com/survey-says-eq-for-the-win-in-2021-beyond-7f8d8b652c8d

8. Lyndsay K.R. Toensing, *The Art of Connected Leadership,* (New York, NY: Morgan James Publishing, 2020), 44.

9. Adele Lynn, *The EQ Difference: A Powerful Plan for Putting Emotional Intelligence to Work*, (New York: American Management Association, 2005), 61.

10. Connie Dieken, *Talk Less, Say More*. (New York, NY: John Wiley and Sons, 2009), p. 22.

11. Emily Sachs, "Paging All Healthcare Practitioners!" *Toastmasters International,* June 2021, https://www.toastmasters.org/magazine/magazine-issues/2021/june/tms-in-healthcare

12. Michael Hoppe, *Active Listening: Improve Your Ability to Listen and Lead*, (Kindle ebook version), (Greensboro, NC: Center for Creative Learning), p. 59.

13. Judith Humphrey, *Speaking As a Leader*, (Ontario: John Wiley & Sons Canada, LTD), 51.

14. Robert Benson, "Ego and Leadership—How to Address Ego in the Workplace" YouTube, November 27, 2018, https://www.youtube.com/watch?v=cGtaPBCeOIw

15. Ibid.

Chapter 6

1. Dr. Karissa Thacker, *The Art Of Authenticity*, (New Jersey: John Wiley and Sons, Inc., 2016), 261–263.

2. WOUB Public Media, July 28, 2020, "Code-Switching Is a Form of Systemic Racism Against Blacks." https://woub.org/2020/07/28/code-switching-is-a-form-of-systemic-racism-against-blacks/

3. Ibid.

4. Courtney L. McCluney, Katharina Robotham, Serenity Lee, Richard Smith, and Myles Durkee, "The Costs of Code-Switching," *Harvard Business Review*, The Big Idea Series, November 15, 2019, https://hbr.org/2019/11/the-costs-of-codeswitching

5. Chandra Arthur, "The Cost of Code Switching," TEDxOrlando, August 22, 2017, https://youtu.be/Bo3hRq2RnNI

6. Ibid.

7. Ibid.

8. Justin Roberson, "Code Switch or Code Break," TEDx Iowa State University, August 21, 2018, https://www.youtube.com/watch?v=dQG8hnShsfY

9. Brené Brown, *Daring Greatly: How the Courage to Be Vulnerable Transforms the Way We Live, Love, Parent, and Lead*, (Kindle ebook version), (New York, NY: Avery Books, 2015), 2.

Chapter 7

1. NPR, June 18, 2020,"How I Built Resilience: Live with Cathy Hughes." https://www.npr.org/2020/06/17/879227259/how-i-built-resilience-live-with-cathy-hughes

2. Ibid.

3. NPR, December 22, 2020, "How I Built This With Guy Raz: Janice Bryant Howroyd 2018," https://www.npr.org/2020/12/22/949258732/actone-group-janice-bryant-howroyd-2018

4. MacMillan Dictionary, Definition of "ambiguity," https://www.macmillandictionary.com/us/dictionary/american/ambiguity

5. Cheryl Cran, *The Art Of Change Leadership*, (New York, NY: John Wiley and Sons, Inc., 2016), 40, 69, 75.

6. Center for Creative Leadership, November 18, 2020, "Are You Facing a Problem? Or a Polarity?" https://www.ccl.org/articles/leading-effectively-articles/are-you-facing-a-problem-or-a-polarity/

7. Kweilin Ellingrud, et al., "Diverse employees are struggling the most during COVID-19: Here's how companies can respond," McKinsey & Company, November 17, 2020, https://www.mckinsey.com/featured-insights/diversity-and-inclusion/diverse-employees-are-struggling-the-most-during-covid-19-heres-how-companies-can-respond

8. Ibid.

9. McKinsey & Company, March 8, 2021, "Seven charts that show COVID-19's Impact on Women's Employment," https://www.mckinsey.com/featured-insights/diversity-and-inclusion/seven-charts-that-show-covid-19s-impact-on-womens-employment

10. Ruchika Tulshyan, "Return to Office?: Some Women of Color Aren't Ready," *New York Times*, June 23, 2021, https://www.nytimes.com/2021/06/23/us/return-to-office-anxiety.html

11. Ibid.

12. Ibid.

Chapter 8

1. Tom Starner, "Study: Workplace Accountability Requires a Specific Strategy," HR Dive, June 2, 2015, https://www.hrdive.com/news/study-workplace-accountability-requires-a-specific-strategy/400130/

2. Kirsten Weir, "More than job satisfaction: Psychologists are discovering what makes work meaningful—and how to create value in any job," American Psychological Association, December 2013, https://www.apa.org/monitor/2013/12/job-satisfaction

3. Partners in Leadership, 2009, *Achieving Results Through Greater Accountability*, https://www.fmi.org/docs/fc_presentations/building_an_accountable_culture_white_paper.pdf?sfvrsn=2

4. FranklinCovey, "The 8th Habit: Big Rocks—Stephen Covey," https://resources.franklincovey.com/the-8th-habit/big-rocks-stephen-r-covey

5. Dave Smith, "The Steve Jobs Guide to Manipulating People and Getting What You Want," *Business Insider*, November 1, 2014, https://www.businessinsider.com/the-steve-jobs-guide-to-manipulating-people-and-getting-what-you-want-2014-10

6. Jim Collins, *Good to Great: Why Some Companies Make the Leap and Others Don't*, (New York: Harper Collins, 2001)

7. John Doerr, *Measure What Matters: How Google, Bono, and the Gates Foundation Rock*, (New York, NY: Penguin Random House, 2018), 7.

8. Ibid.

Chapter 9

1. Carla Harris, *Strategize to Win: The New Way to Start Out, Step Up, or Start Over in Your Career*, (New York, Avery, 2014)

2. WCBI News, December 9, 2019, "Why There Are So Few Blacks in Top Corporate Jobs," https://www.wcbi.com/why-there-are-so-few-blacks-in-top-corporate-jobs/

3. Carla Harris, "How to Find the Person Who Can Help You Get Ahead at Work," TED Talks, January 9, 2019, https://www.youtube.com/watch?v=gpE_W50OTUc

4. Carla Harris, "Building Relationship Currency in an Isolated Environment," LinkedIn, August 26, 2020, https://www.linkedin.com/pulse/building-relationship-currency-isolated-environment-carla-harris

5. John C. Maxwell, *21 Irrefutable Laws of Leadership*, (Tennessee: Thomas Nelson Publishing, 2007), 11–23.

Chapter 10

1. Carla Harris, "How to Find the Person Who Can Help You Get Ahead at Work," TED Talks, January 9, 2019, https://www.youtube.com/watch?v=gpE_W50OTUc

2. Ibid.

3. Chantal Brine, "Why Mentorship Matters: En Point Mentorship Monthly Recap #1," LinkedIn, February 3, 2021, https://www.linkedin.com/pulse/why-mentorship-matters-en-point-monthly-recap-1-chantal-brine/

4. Minda Harts, *The Memo: What Women of Color Need to Know to Secure a Seat at the Table*, (New York, NY: Seal Press, 2020), 19–41.

5. Nick Nelson (founder of The BRANDPRENUER Agency®), in discussion with the author, November 2021.

6. Richard Orbe-Austin, "Why Leadership Programs Are Failing BIPOC Women and How to Truly Support Their Career Advancement," LinkedIn, March 25, 2021, https://www.linkedin.com/pulse/why-leadership-programs-failing-bipoc-women-how-truly-richard

Chapter 11

1. CBS News, *60 Minutes*, Bill Whitaker, January 9, 2022, "The Great Resignation: Why more Americans are quitting their jobs than ever before," https://www.cbsnews.com/news/great-resignation-60-minutes-2022-01-10/

2. Christopher Zara, "The Great Resignation: Here's a Simple Reason Why Your Employees Might Want to Quit," Fast Company, January 26, 2022, https://www.fastcompany.com/90716203/the-great-resignation-heres-a-simple-reason-why-your-employees-want-to-quit

3. Gary Chapman, *Rising Above a Toxic Workplace: Taking Care of Yourself in an Unhealthy Environment*, (Illinois: Northfield Publishing, 2014), 31–49, 129–169.

4. Ibid.

5. Volusia County, Florida, "Dr. Mary McLeod Bethune," https://www.volusia.org/residents/history/volusia-stories/dr-mary-mcleod-bethune.stml

Chapter 12

1. Mayo Clinic, "Depression in Women: Understanding the Gender Gap," January 29, 2019, https://www.mayoclinic.org/diseases-conditions/depression/in-depth/depression/art-20047725

2. Michelle Obama, *Becoming*, (New York: Crown Publishing Group, 2018), 204, 207.

3. *Psychology Today*, Definition of "burnout," https://www.psychologytoday.com/us/basics/burnout

4. Cengage Group, January 20, 2022, "What's Driving the Great Resignation? Pay, Burnout and Stalled Career Growth, According to Cengage Group Research," https://www.cengagegroup.com/news/press-releases/2022/great-resigners-research-report/

5. Terri Ferguson, LCSW, in discussion with the author, December 2021, and Solution Savvy Counseling and Training, https://solutionsavvyllc.com/

6. Angela Duckworth, *Grit: The Power of Passion and Perseverance*, (New York, NY: Scribner Book Company, 2016), 8.

7. Indeed for Employees, Indeed Editorial Team, February 22, 2019, "Why Grit Is Important in Hiring—and How to Identify It," https://www.indeed.com/lead/hire-for-grit

8. Terri Ferguson, LCSW (founder of Solution Savvy Counseling and Training), in discussion with the author, December 2021.

9. Ibid.

.

CPSIA information can be obtained
at www.ICGtesting.com
Printed in the USA
BVHW071513270123
657291BV00005B/1096

9 798986 873008